FORTY-SEVEN
ENCINO TARZANA BRANCH LIBRARY
18231 VENTURA BLVD.
TARZANA, CALIF. 91356

MAKERS OF AMERICA

RICHARD M. NIXON

The Complex President

MARTIN S. GOLDMAN

92 N736Go

Facts On File, Inc.

Richard M. Nixon: The Complex President

Copyright © 1998 by Martin S. Goldman

All rights reserved. No part of this book may be reproduced or utilized in any form or by any means, electronic or mechanical, including photocopying, recording, or by any information storage or retrieval systems, without permission in writing from the publisher. For information contact:

Facts On File, Inc.
11 Penn Plaza
New York NY 10001

Library of Congress Cataloging-in-Publication Data

Goldman, Martin S.
    Richard M. Nixon : the complex president / Martin S. Goldman.
      p. cm. — (Makers of America)
    Includes bibliographical references (p.) and index.
    ISBN 0-8160-3397-8
    1. Nixon, Richard M. (Richard Milhous), 1913– . 2. Presidents—United States—Biography. 3. United States—Politics and government—1945–1989. I. Title. II. Series: Makers of America (Facts on File, Inc.)
E856.G65   1997
973.924'092—dc21
[B]   97-19928

Facts On File books are available at special discounts when purchased in bulk quantities for businesses, associations, institutions or sales promotions. Please call our Special Sales Department in New York at 212/967-8800 or 800/322-8755.

You can find Facts On File on the World Wide Web at
http://www.factsonfile.com

Text design by Cathy Rincon
Cover design by Matt Galemmo

This book is printed on acid-free paper.

Printed in the United States of America

MP FOF 10 9 8 7 6 5 4 3 2 1

CONTENTS

ACKNOWLEDGMENTS v

INTRODUCTION ix

1. BEGINNINGS: NIXON'S EARLY LIFE 1
2. WAR AND POLITICS 11
3. NIXON IN THE NATIONAL ARENA: FROM CONGRESS TO THE SENATE 20
4. FROM SENATOR TO VEEP 32
5. NIXON VERSUS KENNEDY: THE ELECTION OF 1960 49
6. DEFEAT AND RENEWAL: RICHARD NIXON AND THE ELECTION OF 1968 66
7. IN POWER: RICHARD NIXON AND VIETNAM 82
8. WATERGATE I: NIXON, THE ELECTION OF 1972, AND THE BREAK-IN 97
9. WATERGATE II: FROM COVER-UP TO DISGRACE 110
10. FACING HISTORY: RICHARD NIXON'S LAST CRISIS 128

FURTHER READING 136

INDEX 142

*To the Blessed Memory of
Nan Goldman Praissman
My "Aunt Nan"*

ACKNOWLEDGMENTS

"We know perfectly and fully no truth; because we know not all its connections and respects."

—Robert Boyle, 1627–1691

On a warm August morning in 1974—the morning of the steamy day on which Richard Nixon was to leave the presidency and helicopter off into his own private hell of exile and political oblivion—Peter Lisagor, a crusty veteran *Chicago Daily News* reporter, rushed across Lafayette Park toward the White House. There were other reporters scurrying in the same direction that morning, including Tom Brokaw and Dan Rather, who were covering the White House for their respective television networks.

But I especially remember Lisagor because he seemed to be wearing a smirk of self-satisfaction. Peter Lisagor hated Richard Nixon. Lisagor had covered Nixon since the days when Nixon served in the House. He had witnessed numerous Nixon incarnations: earnest young pol; ardent anticommunist; prevaricating senatorial candidate; cold warrior and McCarthyite of the worst stripe; defeated presidential candidate; victorious presidential candidate; president; and, most recently, Watergate scoundrel and (possibly) felon.

As Lisagor passed by I caught his eye. Realizing that I was about to become an intimate eyewitness to an important event in our history—the first resignation of an American president—I couldn't allow him to pass without cracking wise. After all, Lisagor and I were soulmates. We both despised Nixon. And this was to be the day for which we had both been waiting for a long time. "What do you think [CBS News analyst] Eric Sevareid would say? Where is the guy when we need him?" I quipped. Lisagor looked at me briefly and glared. Then he snapped, "How the hell should I know, kid? If you're trying to be funny, this isn't a very funny day!"

Lisagor was right. It wasn't a very funny day. Or a very happy one. It has taken me years of thinking and study to understand what Peter Lisagor meant back then.

I had come to Washington as a mid-level staffer for the American Revolution Bicentennial Commission, but I was hardly a Nixonite. In 1960 I had voted for the first time, and with great optimism, for John F. Kennedy. Years later, as a veteran and young academic, I taught and protested against the war in Vietnam. In May 1970 I marched around the White House during the wave of national unrest that followed the U.S. incursion into Cambodia and the tragic killing of innocent students at Kent State. I had even braved the cruel early November snows of 1972, working in central Massachusetts in the presidential campaign to oust Richard Nixon and elect George McGovern. I saw McGovern as one of the most principled men in the long history of this nation's politics. McGovern took Massachusetts—and lost every other state in the country. How, I wondered in the pain of that election night, could the entire country choose a man like Nixon over McGovern?

Then, by a strange twist of the academic fates, from 1973 to 1975 I found myself not only working for the Nixon administration but actually liking a good many of the people I met in Washington. A lot of those people happened to be Republicans. That is when things started to get very confusing. I had always been led to believe that the Republicans were the bad guys. As I matured and began to read deeper in American political history, I began to understand better what Thomas Jefferson meant in his first inaugural address when he told the American people, "We are all Republicans—we are all Federalists."

Indeed, the strength of the American experiment with democracy is the remarkable fact that we Americans are really all so much alike. The truth is, if we remove the extremes at either end of the political spectrum, Americans are not all that far apart when it comes to most issues. Throughout our history, we have clearly divided over some of the great political debates that characterized each era—expansion; slavery; gold versus silver; farm versus city; too much government; too little government; war; peace; civil rights; and abortion (to name a few).

But these divisions have ultimately been settled, for the most part, and the secret of our success lies in the fact that Jefferson was right: whichever party we support, we all believe in the value of our democratic republic. That is why Peter Lisagor understood far better than I that August 9, 1974, was a very sad day for our country. A president had failed and failed dismally. And we Americans were all the poorer.

Richard Nixon is probably the most hated president of the 20th century (if not in all of American history). His many detractors really do despise him, and his champions have been few. Yet it can be argued that no president since Franklin D. Roosevelt has made such an impact. Had Nixon lasted a full two terms there is little doubt that his impact would have been even greater. Love him or hate him, no one can argue with the notion that Richard Nixon has stamped his name indelibly on the latter part of this century's history.

I don't hate Nixon anymore. And I certainly don't love him. That is, perhaps, why I wanted to do a book on Nixon. I used to ask the students in my course on the presidency of John F. Kennedy at Boston University how many would have signed up for a course on Richard Nixon. Out of 75 to 100 students, only a few hands would go up each semester. Although they were too young to recall much about Nixon's presidency, the feelings of many of their Nixon-hating teachers had clearly influenced their thinking. They could hardly have been expected to know that Richard Nixon's influence on American life was far greater than that of the martyred John F. Kennedy. Poor Nixon! Even dead, he was still up against his archrival and was still running second. John F. Kennedy will always be sexier than Richard Nixon. But he will never be as important.

When my former editor James Warren suggested I write a book on Nixon as a follow-up to my study *John F. Kennedy: Portrait of a President* (Facts On File, 1995), the suggestion made a lot of sense. It is my hope that this work will inspire students to dig much deeper into the life and times of this tragic, brilliant, complex, fascinating (and, at times, mean-spirited and vile) personality whose life has had such a strong impact on our times.

This study wouldn't exist without the support and encouragement of two people who have been vital to my success as a scholar, teacher, and writer: Michael and Carol Kort. Michael Kort teaches history at Boston University and Carol is an accomplished writer in her own right. I love and value them both.

There are a number of people at Merrimack College who have become trusted colleagues and treasured friends, beginning with President Richard J. Santagati, a great academic leader and a valued friend. Without Padraic O'Hare, whose irrepressible Irish/Jewish spirit and collegial style combines what is best about academic life, I wouldn't have had the opportunity to teach, work, and thrive in an extraordinary community of students and scholars. He is a dear and wonderful friend. Reverend Thomas Casey has become a trusted colleague and friend as chair of Merrimack's Religious Studies Department. Also, my thanks to my hardworking administrative assistant, Gail Farmer. To all my other colleagues and close friends at Merrimack College (they are too numerous to mention) who have supported what we've been trying to accomplish for two years, my sincere gratitude.

To my two Larrys: Larry Lowenthal in Boston and Larry Laster in Philadelphia.

To Ann Marchette, for all the support and love over my Sudbury years.

My thanks to my editors at Facts On File, Nicole Bowen and John Anthony Scott.

To Gideon, my Labrador retriever, who never fails to make me smile.

And finally, to my very supportive family: my parents, Ruth and Louis Goldman, whose love has always been there without qualification; my brother Ken Goldman; and my aunt Nan Praissman, to whom this book is dedicated and who died on March 7, 1997. She was one of the important teachers in my life.

INTRODUCTION

"I hereby resign the Office of President of the United States."

On August 9, 1974, the news from Washington left the American people reeling. For the second time in little over a decade they had lost their leader. On November 22, 1963, President John F. Kennedy had been assassinated in Dallas, Texas. On the night of August 8, 1974, President Richard M. Nixon, the 37th president of the United States, became the first chief executive to announce that he would give up the powerful office for which he had fought so hard his entire political life.

Nixon had invited riends and supporters, 20 senators and 26 congressmen, for a farewell meeting in the Cabinet Room. Describing that meeting, Barry Goldwater, the Republican senator from Arizona said, "He just told us that the country couldn't operate with a half-time President. Then he broke down and cried and he had to leave the room. Then the rest of us broke down and cried."

Shortly after 9:00 EST, Nixon broke the news to a stunned and bewildered nation in what the *Washington Post* described as "a subdued yet dramatic television address from the Oval Office."

He told a national and worldwide audience,

> In the past few days . . . it has become evident to me that I no longer have a strong enough political base in the Congress to justify continuing that effort. As long as there was such a base, I felt strongly that it was necessary to see the constitutional process through to its conclusion, that to do otherwise would be unfaithful to the spirit of that deliberately difficult process, and a dangerously destabilizing precedent for the future.

But with the disappearance of that base, I now believe that the constitutional purpose has been served, and there is no longer a need for the process to be prolonged.

Then Nixon, who had never been very comfortable under the white-hot scrutiny of the television cameras and bright lights, looked directly into the cameras and said, "Therefore, I shall resign the presidency effective at noon tomorrow."

In what had become a trademark of Richard Nixon's public life, he attempted, even in his last dark moment of power, to put a public relations spin on his humiliation and shame: "By taking this action," Nixon continued, "I hope that I will have hastened the start of that process of healing which is so desperately needed in America. I regret deeply any injuries that may have been done in the course of the events that led to this decision. I would say only that if some of my judgments were wrong—and some were wrong—they were made in what I believed at the time to be in the best interest of the nation."

The next morning, at the urging of his senior aide, General Alexander Haig, President Richard M. Nixon signed his name to a sheet of paper containing a single sentence: "I hereby resign the Office of President of the United States." The paper was then delivered, in accordance with the law, to Secretary of State Henry Kissinger, a Nixon appointee who had risen from the position of National Security Adviser to the top foreign policy position in American government under the mentorship of the beleaguered president.

How did it all come to this terrible moment in history for Richard M. Nixon? The rise and fall of Richard Milhous Nixon is a historic tale of truly Shakespearean proportions. Like Hamlet and Macbeth, Nixon was a many-sided character. To say that he was a complex man is an understatement. Richard Nixon was an enigma—a puzzle. Scholars and historians will be attempting to find the keys to that puzzle for many years to come.

Nixon had served 2,026 days in office since his election in 1968. He had served as vice president under Dwight David Eisenhower from 1953 to 1960. Then, after losing the presidency in 1960 to John F. Kennedy in a very close race and suffering defeat in the California gubernatorial election of 1962, Nixon had angrily announced his retirement from active political life. Yet, in the wake of assassinations, urban riots, and campus upheavals over the war in Vietnam, Nixon had returned to the political fray, successfully vied for the Republican presidential nomination, and narrowly triumphed over his Democratic rival, Vice President Hubert H. Humphrey, in the 1968 election.

As president, although never popular with the press and the university elites he despised, Nixon had successfully negotiated nuclear nonproliferation treaties with the Russians (the famous SALT—Strategic Arms Limitation Talk treaties); begun a winding down of American involvement in the quagmire of the Vietnam War—a military adventure started under the presidency of John F. Kennedy; and, even though he prided himself in being a leading anticommunist cold warrior, had begun to open the doors to the People's Republic of China.

As his second term began, Richard Nixon was poised for greatness, even though he had never been a popular leader or a particularly warm human being. But then it all began to unravel. The Watergate scandal, like a giant octopus, spread its tentacles to ensnare everyone even remotely involved. What appeared at first to be a petty controversy had wrapped itself around a petty man. And in the end, the presidency of Richard Nixon was destroyed.

In his August 8 speech the American people got a chance to appreciate Nixon's leadership qualities when he stated that on taking office he had made a "sacred commitment" to "consecrate my office and wisdom to the cause of peace among nations." Nixon had demonstrated the force of that pledge during the October 1973 Yom Kippur War when his secretary of state shuttled between Israel and Egypt working to bring about a cease-fire and then some possibility of accord. While Henry Kissinger's "shuttle diplomacy" did not bring about a permanent peace between the warring Middle East nations, it set the peace process on a course to later success. As Nixon put it,

> I have done my very best in all the days since to be true to that pledge. This more than anything is what I hoped to achieve when I sought the presidency. This more than anything is what I hope will be my legacy to you, to our country, as I leave the presidency.

"A President's power begins slipping away the moment it is known that he is going to leave," Richard Nixon later recalled. On Friday, August 9, 1974, Nixon readied himself to hand over power and leave office. With his vice president, former congressman Gerald Ford, poised to succeed him, all Nixon had to do was say farewell and leave Washington with as much dignity as he could possibly maintain at this dark moment of disgrace.

Instead, with his tearful staff and distraught family surrounding him, Richard Nixon made his last political exit the most painful of his long career. As he fought back what he later called "A flood tide of emotions," Nixon offered a convoluted and disjointed address to those loyalists who had served him over the years and to the nation at large. From the East Room in the White House, an obviously exhausted and distraught president gave a meandering farewell talk. He quoted a tribute former president Theodore Roosevelt had made to his first wife (Nixon's point was that Roosevelt had remained in the political arena despite his setbacks) and launched into a nostalgic reminiscence about his own impoverished parents and their diligent struggle to maintain their dignity under adverse conditions in pre–depression era California. For Richard Nixon, "This was the nightmare end of a long dream. I had come so far from the little house in Yorba Linda to the great house in Washington."

Finally, after a maudlin reference to his sainted mother, Nixon's ordeal was over. Accompanied by President Ford and Ford's wife Betty, the former president walked down a long red carpet under a canopy to the steps of Marine One, the presidential helicopter.

Raising his arms in the familiar Nixon salute, Richard Nixon, the 37th president of the United States, flew off into history. He would later recall his wife Pat, faithful to her husband to the very end, saying, "It's so sad. It's so sad."

Bruce Mazlish, a Nixon scholar who sees psychology as one key to unlocking the mystery of Richard Nixon, wrote in his book *In Search of Nixon*,

> With the explosion of the first atomic bomb at Alamogordo, New Mexico, on July 16, 1945, the office of President of the United States assumed an awesome new importance not

only for this country, but also for the rest of the world. As the office became more important, so did the person occupying it.

Ever since Harry Truman had made the difficult decision to drop the first atomic bomb on Japan to end World War II, every president of the United States, as titular leader of the most powerful nation in the free world, had had the power to kill every single person on the planet. A presidential decision could place American combat troops in the field at the drop of a hat; a wrong decision could cost the lives of hundreds of thousands. And between 1945 and the end of the presidency of Richard Nixon, many wrong decisions had been made at the presidential level.

Richard M. Nixon had made his share of those wrong decisions. But he had also made some correct ones. Who was Richard Nixon? Where did he come from and how did he arrive on the American political scene? More important, what made him tick? What dark forces within Nixon led him to subvert the Constitution of the United States by betraying the trust implicitly placed in his high office, resulting in the greatest presidential scandal in all of American history—the Watergate crimes and cover-up that included the blatant misuse of government agencies such as the FBI (Federal Bureau of Investigation), the CIA (Central Intelligence Agency), and the IRS (Internal Revenue Service)?

In the end, the quest for answers will be more than just a search for Richard Nixon. It may well be a search for the heart and soul of America.

1
BEGINNINGS
Nixon's Early Life

"I was born in a house my father built."

Richard Milhous Nixon was born on January 9, 1913, in the modest farming community of Yorba Linda, California, some 30 miles southeast of Los Angeles. It was a small town of 200 people where the local farmers grew avocados, citrus fruits, barley, and alfalfa. Yorba Linda was, as Nixon himself recalled, an "idyllic" setting, with the springlike air always heavy with the fragrant smell of orange blossoms.

Richard Nixon was the second son of Frank and Hannah Nixon. Frank Nixon had originally moved to California in order to recover from a severe case of frostbite he had gotten while working as a motorman on an open trolley in Columbus, Ohio. In 1908, when he met Hannah Milhous, Frank Nixon was living in Whittier and was still driving a trolley. "We can assume," Bruce Mazlish has wryly noted, "that Frank Nixon had married above his station."

Nixon's mother, Hannah, came from a hard-working, pious, and comfortably middle-class Quaker family. Nixon's brother Harold was born in 1909. After the birth of Richard, three more children followed: Donald in 1914, Arthur in 1918, and Edward

The Nixon family: Frank, Hannah, and from left to right, Harold, Donald, and Richard (Richard Nixon Library)

in 1930. Years later, when Nixon looked back on his childhood, he saw his early years in romantic, nostalgic, and almost mythical terms. Although the Nixon family had certainly struggled and their life was not easy, things were no different for hundreds of thousands of other Americans who came of age in those times.

When he became a public person, Nixon wanted people to think of him as a young Abraham Lincoln—a poor boy who, embodying the American dream, had pulled himself up by his own bootstraps. But young Richard Nixon was no Lincoln, and Yorba Linda, California, was a far cry from the rugged frontier of Lincoln's time. To perpetuate this comparison, Nixon would write in his memoirs, "Our life in Yorba Linda was hard but happy. My father worked at whatever jobs he could find."

Richard's father, Francis (Frank) Anthony Nixon, was born on a farm in Ohio in 1878. He had a difficult childhood. His mother died of tuberculosis when he was seven, and his stepmother beat him. For most of his life he had been something of a failure. In 1922, after planting a lemon grove that failed in Yorba Linda, Frank Nixon moved his family to Whittier, California, where he opened a general store and gas station. Young Richard worked at the counter and pumped gas.

Frank Nixon was typical of an entire generation of Americans who, in the early years of the 20th century, had headed to the West Coast lured by the warm sunshine and the good life, as they pursued their American dream. They saw California as a golden opportunity to get their slice of a growing American pie in the first decades of a new century. For many of them the dream had turned into a nightmare.

According to people who knew him, Frank Nixon had a volatile and unpredictable personality. In scholar Fawn M. Brodie's opinion, he "did not become less surly and disagreeable when he was no longer poor." Bruce Mazlish is more charitable and writes that "[Frank] Nixon seems to have been a good man in a family dominated by strong women."

Nixon's mother, born Hannah Milhous, was a dedicated Quaker with strong pacifist views. Her family had moved to California from Indiana. The Milhouses, with roots in County Kildare, Ireland, had come to Pennsylvania in 1729 in search of religious freedom. Both the Nixon and Milhous families had deep roots in American history. One forefather had crossed the

Delaware with General Washington during the Revolution. Another was killed at Gettysburg in the fiercest battle of the Civil War.

Hannah Milhous Nixon worked long and hard to lift her family out of its early years of poverty and want. She was extremely fastidious in her manners and dress and clearly had a marked impact on the childhood of her second son. As Richard Nixon's first-grade teacher recalled, "Every day, he wore a freshly starched white shirt with a big black bow tie and knee pants. He always looked like his mother had scrubbed him from head to toe. The funny thing is, I never remember him ever getting dirty."

Richard Nixon variously remembered his mother as "a saint," as a "very strong woman," and as a woman "of great strength of character." Even when he entered politics, Nixon would recall,

> The last thing my mother, a devout Quaker, wanted me to do was go into the warfare of politics. I recall she once expressed the hope that I might become a missionary to our Quaker mission fields in Central America. But true to her Quaker tradition she never tried to force me in the direction she herself might have preferred.

As a child Richard had a number of brushes with death. At age three he narrowly escaped being killed when he fell out of a horse-drawn buggy and was grazed by the heavy wheel before his mother could rein in the horse. The accident left him with an ugly scar that ran from above his forehead all the way down to his neck.

After that, it seemed that young Richard was always coming down with one illness or another. At four he nearly died of pneumonia, and in his senior year of high school a severe attack of undulant fever brought his temperature to 104 degrees for over a week and caused his absence from school for much of that year.

There is a strong possibility that, in his mind, his mother had failed him in his crucial formative years. Although this failure may be partially tied to two major tragedies that devastated the Nixon family before young Richard turned 20, Nixon's relationship with his mother—a key to understanding the person he became—was strongly affected.

In 1925, when Richard was 12, his younger brother Arthur died of tubercular encephalitis. Richard was close to Arthur, loved him very much, and was scarred by his untimely death. While Hannah Nixon seemed to accept Arthur's death stoically as "one of the ways of the Lord," Nixon recalled that the words "tubercular encephalitis . . . were too big, too cold, and too impersonal for us to grasp or understand. . . . For weeks after Arthur's funeral there was not a day that I did not think about him and cry."

To further encumber Nixon's early years, when the eldest Nixon boy, Harold, became ill with tuberculosis at about the same time Arthur died, his mother took him to Arizona in the hope of curing him in the fresh air. During this period the other Nixons remained in California; the boys took turns with their father preparing meals and running the household. Under great financial pressure, Frank Nixon was able to pay the family's huge medical bills only by selling off half the land on which his store was located. As one Nixon biographer has written, "It was a period of extreme hardship for the whole family."

During this time, when Richard was about 12, some scholars claim he was "abandoned" by Hannah Nixon when she spent two years caring for Harold in Arizona. Though words like *abandon*, *betrayal*, *desertion*, and *domineering* seem a bit harsh and psychologically overdrawn to describe what Hannah Nixon felt she had to do in the midst of a desperate family crisis, young Richard may have been deeply affected by the absence of his mother. When Hannah, convinced that her son had musical talent, sent Richard away to live for five months with his aunt Jane Beeson, a music teacher, it is likely, as one historian has claimed, that he felt "abandoned, pushed out of the family." But if he held it against his mother, Richard did an excellent job of hiding his feelings. He certainly did not hesitate to join Harold and Hannah during the summer after his high school graduation in Prescott, Arizona, where he took a job as a barker in the Slippery Gulch Rodeo.

Did Richard Nixon resent his mother for all the attention she lavished on his sicker siblings? Did he suffer great anxiety and a sense of abandonment as a result of her extended absences?

It's hard to say. Clearly, the long absence of his mother during his formative years had to have some effect on him and on the rest of the family. But it is a stretch to imagine that these tragic events made the Nixons a dysfunctional family. For comparison, consider the long parental absences suffered by the young Kennedys growing up in Massachusetts.

As he grew older, more mature, and thus better able to view his mother's actions from a more informed perspective, Richard must have realized that Hannah's attention to his younger and

Richard Nixon is Number 12 on the Whittier College football team.
(Whittier College)

older brother was necessitated by the critical nature of their illnesses. Certainly, there was a vast difference between her actions and the extended travels of the wealthy Kennedys. (Rose Kennedy would go off to Europe for months at a time to sightsee and shop; Joe Kennedy would always be away on business). In any case, Hannah Nixon's efforts were ultimately in vain; after years of special care, Harold Nixon died in 1933, when Richard was about 19. Clearly, the deaths of his brothers were pivotal events that shaped Nixon's early life in addition to determining his relationship with his mother. One of Richard's first girlfriends, Ola Welch Jobe, observed that Hannah was "a lovely lady, wonderful to me, but an iron fist in a velvet glove." Still, Jobe concluded, Hannah Nixon was "overpowered" by her husband Frank.

At the age of 17 Richard Nixon entered Whittier College, a local Quaker school. At Whittier he majored in history and won distinction as a champion debater. In his sophomore year Nixon competed in over 50 debates for Whittier, winning most of them, including a match with the national champions. He was able to pay his way through school by operating the fresh-vegetable counter at the family business. Ever the outsider, Nixon was among a small group of Whittier students who formed a new campus fraternity, the Orthagonians (Square Shooters), which competed with the traditional fraternity made up of young men from the wealthier families. Nixon also played on the football team in his freshman year although, according to one classmate, "Dick had two left feet. He couldn't coordinate."

Nixon is remembered at Whittier as a diligent and serious student who seems to have been popular and well liked. He was elected president of his freshman class and was known as a campus leader. One of his close friends, Orthagonian fraternity brother William Brock, recalled Nixon fondly: "He was little, but he had more fight and spunk than the big man." Years later, when Nixon became a public figure, Brock, an African American who became a successful electrical engineer (and usually voted for Democrats), spoke out forcefully for his old friend: "And I really get mad when I hear Democrats or anybody accuse him of bigotry. That sort of thing is fantastic. Dick was my buddy in college many years before he or anybody else figured him to become a politician. He was one of the fellows who got me into the Orthagonians."

In 1934 Nixon graduated second in his class at Whittier. Although he would have preferred studying law at Harvard, financial considerations forced him to accept a $200 scholarship to Duke University's newly established law school.

When he arrived in Durham, North Carolina, in the fall of 1934, the United States was in the midst of the Great Depression. For the first two years of school Nixon lived in a rented room for which he paid the princely sum of $5 a month. With an allowance of only $35 a month from his still financially strapped family, Nixon took a job for 35 cents an hour doing research in the law library in one of the many New Deal programs established under the auspices of the National Youth Administration.

Nixon looked back on his law school years at Duke with great fondness. He said,

> My three years at Duke provided an excellent legal background. Despite the fact that we had some intense discussions on the race issue, and while I could not agree with many of my Southern classmates on this subject, I learned in these years to understand and respect them for their patriotism, their pride, and their enormous interest in national issues.

In 1937, after graduating third in his class, Nixon returned to Whittier. He had flirted briefly with the idea of a career in J. Edgar Hoover's Federal Bureau of Investigation (FBI) after Dean H. Claude Horack wrote Hoover that "Mr. Richard Nixon is one of the finest young men . . . that I have ever had in my classes. He is a very superior student, alert, aggressive, a fine speaker and one who can do an exceptionally good piece of research when called on to do so." But just before his application was processed for final acceptance as a "G-Man," the FBI appropriation was cut, and, as fate would have it, Richard Nixon stayed in California. After some weeks of intensive study, Nixon passed the state bar exam and took a position with the oldest law firm in Whittier—Wright and Bewley. He did estate and divorce work but didn't particularly enjoy the domestic practice, which he found "unhappy and unsettling."

Still, Nixon enjoyed being a lawyer, and his name was soon added to the firm, which became Wright, Bewley, and Nixon. As Nixon recalled, "Now for the first time I was no longer Frank and Hannah Nixon's son—I was Mr. Nixon, the new partner in Wright and Bewley."

In addition to his new practice, Nixon kept himself busy in the community. He served as a trustee of Whittier College, was president of the college alumni association, was a member of the Twenty-Thirty Club (a junior chamber of commerce), and acted in a little theater group. Nixon's theatrical aspirations finally led to the great romance of his life.

In the winter of 1938, after trying out for a part in a play, Nixon was introduced to Thelma Catherine "Pat" Ryan, a pretty red-headed high school teacher. "I found I could not take my eyes away from her," he recalled.

Pat Ryan had been born in the stark copper mining town of Ely, Nevada, on March 16, 1912. Her Irish father had traveled west from Connecticut and finally settled in Artesia, a small town 20 miles southwest of Los Angeles. After an impoverished childhood (both her parents had died by the time she turned 17), Pat went to New York, where she took a summer course at Columbia University in 1932. The next year she returned to California to enter the University of Southern California, graduating in 1937 with honors. Nixon courted the vivacious high school teacher for two years before he was able to convince her to marry him. As Pat Nixon later said, "On our first date he told me he was going to marry me, but I wasn't ready to settle down." Nevertheless, they were married in a Quaker ceremony on June 21, 1940, just as the dark clouds of the war in Europe began to hover over the United States. That fall Nixon supported the Republican candidate for the presidency. He recalled, "I strongly supported Wendell Willkie because, while I favored some of Roosevelt's domestic programs, particularly Social Security, I opposed his attempt to break the two-term tradition." (In 1940 Franklin D. Roosevelt had decided to make an unprecedented third run for the presidency.)

In 1942 the young couple moved to Washington, D.C., where Nixon took a job with the Office of Price Administration (OPA), one of the many government agencies created by the Roosevelt administration after the United States declared war on Germany and Japan in December 1941. As

Nixon rationalized his decision to serve in the government controlled by Roosevelt and the New Deal Democrats, "it seemed a good opportunity to go to Washington and observe the working of the government firsthand." In addition, Hannah Nixon was worried that her son would be forced to violate his Quaker faith by entering the armed services. Clearly, as his mother saw it, a government position was far more desirable. But Nixon soon grew restless as a bureaucrat dealing with such matters as the rationing of rubber and automobile tires. He despised the German dictator Adolf Hitler and was eager to make a contribution in the war effort despite his Quaker upbringing. Thus, when Nixon heard that young lawyers were being recruited as officers by the navy, he applied for a commission. In August 1942 he found himself at Quonset Point, Rhode Island, for training as a naval officer. At the age of 29, like other young men of his generation, Richard M. Nixon said good-bye to his loved ones and went off to war.

2
WAR AND POLITICS

"Dear Dick. I am writing you this short note to ask if you would like to be a candidate for Congress on the Republican ticket in 1946."

—H. L. Perry

One recent study of Richard Nixon's life places heavy emphasis on Nixon's wartime service. According to Jonathan Aitken, "Richard Nixon's three and a half years' service in the US Navy were important to the formation of his character."

However, if any words can accurately describe Richard Nixon's wartime experiences they would probably be tedious and boring. In a letter to his parents on November 1, 1942, Nixon himself indicates his distaste for the tediousness of military life: "Well here I am, standing a 24-hour Navy Watch in the middle of Iowa!"

Lieutenant JG (Junior Grade) Nixon, who had been promoted from the starting officer's rank of ensign because of his law school background, had not enlisted in the navy in order to spend his time monitoring telephones and teletype messages. He yearned for some excitement and longed to be free of his deskbound shore responsibilities as a communications officer in Ottumwa, Iowa. The only memorable event during those first six months was Nixon's first ride in an airplane—and he became airsick.

Nixon had applied for "Ships and Stations" as his first choice for active duty. He was very unhappy at having been sent to Iowa for service at a naval air station that was still under construction and where the uncompleted runway ended in a cornfield. But Nixon was always something of a pragmatist—someone who could make the best of a bad situation by adjusting himself to the hard realities of life. And so he and Pat, who took a job as a bank teller, settled down to life in the Midwest. But once again fate intervened. As Nixon noted,

> Just when it began to seem that I might be landlocked in Iowa for the rest of the war, I saw a notice that applications for sea duty would be accepted from officers aged twenty-nine or younger. I was exactly twenty-nine and I sent the application immediately.

In May 1943, with Pat's blessing, Nixon got the sea duty for which he had hoped. He shipped out to the Pacific theater as an operations officer with the South Pacific Combat Air Transport Command (SCAT). For the next 15 months Nixon's job was to set up temporary air bases that would be used to get airborne supplies to the remote battle zones as U.S. forces pressed the Japanese in the Pacific. Thus, like many other heroic young Americans of his generation, Nixon found himself jumping from island to island, serving on Guadalcanal, Bougainville, Vella Lavella, and Green Island.

Years later, when he became a successful politician, Nixon tried to appear modest when discussing his record of service in World War II. In what was to become typical of Nixon-speak, he said in 1952,

> My service record was not a particularly unusual one. I went to the South Pacific. I guess I'm entitled to a couple of battle stars. I got a couple of letters of commendation, but I was just there when the bombs were falling.

The reality was that Nixon saw little combat. Except for the time he spent on Bougainville, when the island was bombed for 28 nights, Nixon's outfit was stationed in noncombat fringe areas. One of Nixon's wartime comrades remembered him as a hard-working and self-reliant young commanding officer. Edward J. McCaffrey of Concord, Massachusetts, recalled, "He made an awful lot of sense. He had no more rank than most of us . . . but he commanded a lot of respect from the guys with whom he came in contact. When things got a bit hectic, he never lost his head."

Nixon would never have the chance to become a hero like his political nemesis John F. Kennedy, whose PT boat was cut in half by a Japanese destroyer and whose courageous rescue of his crewmen became the stuff of Hollywood legend (with the help of his father's massive and well-financed public relations machine). But as Fawn M. Brodie wrote, "The Nixon war record required no apology." Among other initiatives, Nixon set up the only hamburger stand in the South Pacific. In the middle of the jungle, exhausted pilots found free coffee, juice, and sandwiches at "Nixon's Snack Shack" on Green Island. To fill out the long and tedious hours of duty with little to do, Nixon, like many navy men, became adept as a poker player. He would often play for hours at a time. As one of his buddies related, "A hundred Navy officers will tell you that Nix never lost a cent at poker." Some observers believe that it was the money he won playing wartime poker that actually enabled Nixon to launch his political career.

Nixon himself, however, downplayed his abilities as a card player:

> My poker playing during this time has been somewhat exaggerated in terms of both my skill and my winnings. In Whittier any kind of gambling had been anathema to me as a Quaker. But the pressures of wartime, and the even more oppressive monotony, made it an irresistible diversion. I found poker playing instructive as well as entertaining and profitable.

Another wartime pal, Lester Wroble, probably came closest to the truth when he noted, "Dick never lost, but he was never a big winner. He always played it cautious and close to the belt. . . . He seemed always to end up a game somewhere between $30 and $60 ahead."

Richard Nixon was never known to be a man with a warm and engaging personality as a public person. But to the men who served under him during the war he was a regular guy, remembered affectionately by his men as "Nick Nixon." When he became famous, some of his military subordinates compared Nixon to the fictional hero Mr. Roberts, the personable, can-do World War II naval officer portrayed by Henry Fonda in the 1955 film of that name and in a prior Broadway play. Like Mr. Roberts, Nixon commanded a diverse group of young Americans, including men of Polish, Irish, and Mexican backgrounds, a Nebraska farmer, and a Native American. To a man, they all had fond memories of Nixon and always saw him as "one of us." As one Nixon biographer has observed, "This rapport between blue-collar Americans and Richard Nixon was an important ingredient in his rise to power."

Like many young men of his generation, Richard Nixon had a chance to view the full reality of horror and brutality that modern warfare could bring to the mid-20th century. Nixon recalled watching a damaged B-29 bomber attempting a crash landing on its belly on a desolate island airstrip. He recorded how he and his men had cheered as the plane appeared initially to make a safe landing. "Then," Nixon wrote, "we watched in horror as it crashed head-on into a bulldozer and exploded. The carnage was terrible. I can still see the wedding ring on the charred hand of one of the crewmen when I carried his body from the twisted wreckage."

To fill the seemingly endless hours when he was off-duty, Nixon also became a voracious reader. He would read anything he could find, from cheap detective thrillers to the Bible. He also kept up, as best he could from the South Pacific, with the news from home. He devoured all the old newspapers and magazines he could get his hands on, including *Time*, *Life*, *Collier's*, and the *New York Times*.

Nixon was very bright and a quick learner. He soon became an avid annotator of the articles he read and would often make detailed notes on subjects that attracted his interest. His attention, perhaps even then with an eye to his political future after the war, usually focused on international affairs. As one of his friends recalled, "Most of us had big grandiose schemes. Dick's plans were concise, concrete and specific."

The tedium of service in the South Pacific for Nixon was finally relieved in the summer of 1944 when he was reassigned and ordered to Alameda, California. With a letter of commendation for his service in SCAT signed by Vice Admiral J. H. Newton, commander of the South Pacific Fleet, Nixon returned to Hawaii on August 3, 1944.

By V-J (Victory over Japan) Day, August 14, 1945, Nixon was holding down a desk job and mulling over navy contracts for the War Department in an office in New York City. He seemed, finally, happily settled down to a steady job in the navy. But the looming prospect of returning to the tedium and boredom inherent in the general practice of law, after the lack of excitement during his wartime service, bore heavily on Nixon's mind and made a legal career very unappealing. Nixon had given several well-received after-dinner speeches to the Southern California Rotary Club, dazzling some of the stodgy old Republican boys with war stories of his time spent in the Solomon Islands. Now that he was in touch with some high-level Republicans in and around Whittier, Nixon began to view politics as a way out of the full-time practice of law. His persistence was rewarded in October 1945 when he received a letter from an old mentor, Herman L. Perry, asking if he would be interested in becoming a candidate for Congress.

Although the Nixons had little money and no rich friends (they had saved $10,000 from Pat's salary and his poker winnings for the down payment on their first home), and even though Pat was pregnant, they threw caution to the winds. As Nixon told his wife, "we won't be much worse off for losing. And if I lose, I'll always have the option of picking up my law practice in Whittier or even going to LA to open up an office. They say running for Congress is good publicity for a lawyer. Let's do it."

Two days later Nixon called Perry, told him that he was honored by the offer, and accepted. The next day he wrote Perry a letter formally confirming his interest in a congressional run, saying, "I feel very strongly that Jerry Voorhis can be beaten and I'd welcome the opportunity to take a crack at him."

For 10 years, Republicans in California's 12th Congressional District, which reached all the way from the brown foothills of southern Los Angeles to the San Gabriel mountains, had been trying to dislodge Representative Jerry Voorhis, a liberal Democrat who had once been a youthful Socialist supporter of Upton Sinclair's EPIC (End Poverty in California) movement. Voorhis, the idealistic son of a millionaire, had been voted "best congressman west of the Mississippi" by the Washington press, but the business interests in California saw him as the worst. He had voted for federal control of the tidelands oil deposits and had helped pass legislation to curtail the profits of banks that sold government bonds.

With the end of World War II and the defeat of fascism, the American people began to turn their attention toward the issue of communism and the growing worldwide power of the Soviet Union. The Voorhis record was clearly anticommunist. Congressman Voorhis had sponsored a law, the Voorhis Act, requiring any organization under the control of a foreign government to register with the Justice Department. He had also fought against Communist infiltration of the American labor movement. Nixon saw Voorhis as "a hard-working and generally respected congressman," but he also felt that Voorhis "was not really in tune with the voters." Years later when he wrote his memoirs, Nixon was still unable to forgive Voorhis for his liberal views. As Nixon wrote,

> Voorhis, the former Socialist, believed in large-scale government intervention and I did not. He saw dark conspiracies among "reactionaries" and "monopolies," and I did not. He was generally an uncritical supporter of the labor unions, while I considered myself their critical friend. He advocated policies that I believed shackled and restricted American industry. His political views were 180 degrees away from mine. Most important, his votes in Congress on a wide range of issues did not represent the wishes of the voters of his district.

Even so, in 1946 Nixon wasn't quite sure what he believed in terms of a political philosophy. When he was initially recruited to run for office, the people drafting him weren't even sure of his party affiliation, though Nixon is alleged to have stated, "I guess I'm a Republican. I voted for [Republican presidential candidate Thomas] Dewey in 1944."

The primary results looked ominous for the new candidate. Voorhis won the Democratic nomination easily and, in the open primary, had polled enough Republican votes to give him a 7,000-vote lead over Nixon. By 1946 the Republican Party, which had once dominated California politics, was on the run. Between 1930 and 1955 the state tripled its population, but with the added population came many more problems. After a decade of depression, drought, war, and unprecedented industrial growth, in 1946 power was up for grabs on the fast political track under the California sunshine. With the seeming success of President Roosevelt's New Deal, Republicans were outnumbered by a million Democratic voters in California. Thus, as William Costello wrote in *The Facts About Nixon*, "It looked as though Nixon could be written off as another loser."

However, Nixon had a secret weapon: Murray Chotiner. Today, Chotiner would be called a "spin doctor." He was the first of a new breed on the postwar American political scene—the political operator. Before the age of television and mass communication, political operators functioned behind closed doors and largely in secret. Today, with millions of dollars to be made by appearing in full public view, political operators in both parties clog up the airwaves and the political process with their well-rehearsed wit and homespun political wisdom. Chotiner, one of the first dirty tricksters in modern American politics, was a jovial, overweight, and apparently harmless presence. But his appearance made it easy to misjudge him. Behind his jolly facade, the Los Angeles lawyer was an angry and aggressive presence on the California political landscape. As Fawn M. Brodie has described him, Chotiner was "the Machiavelli of California politics, master smear artist, and Svengali to Nixon's Trilby." And as historian Garry Wills has written, until Richard Nixon met Chotiner, he was "a fundamentally decent man."

Chotiner convinced Nixon to challenge Voorhis to a series of five public debates. At worst, Chotiner insisted, Nixon would lose; but at best, the debates might set the Nixon campaign on fire. As it turned out, Chotiner was right. Many observers believe that the turning point came in the first debate, over the question of Voorhis's endorsement by the Political Action Committee of the Congress of Industrial Organizations (CIO). A Nixon advertisement taken out before the debate had declared, "A vote for Nixon is a vote against the Communist-dominated PAC with its gigantic slush fund." Voorhis, in his debate with Nixon, vigorously denied either seeking or having the support of the CIO's Political Action Committee. But Nixon, prepared by Chotiner, was ready. He leaped to his feet, produced the text of a document from the Los Angeles chapter of the national

PAC that recommended support of Voorhis, and read off the names of the officers of the national chapter who were also officers of the regional group. Then, with a flair for the dramatic, Nixon thrust the list at his opponent. For the rest of the campaign, Voorhis found himself caught like a fly on flypaper by the sticky question of his ties to the Communists. He issued a long statement noting that while he cherished the support of labor, he didn't want the backing of the California CIO because "under present top leadership of the CIO in California, there is at least grave question whether the Communist Party does not exercise inordinate if not decisive influence over state and county organizations."

Under Chotiner's tutelage, Nixon discovered that a campaign of smears and half-truths could be very effective with a public that kept only one eye on politics and the other on life's everyday problems. Nixon soon spread the word in his campaign ads that Voorhis had been a member of the Socialist Party.

With no record to defend, Nixon could attack Voorhis while promising the voters of California a program of federal tax reduction and assuring them that a Republican Congress would "solve the meat, housing and controls problem." (A number of wartime restrictions were still in effect.) Nixon won the election with a vote of 65,586 to Voorhis's 49,994. He was one of seven Republicans to unseat incumbent Democrats in California in 1946, as the Republican Party won control of the 80th Congress. In Nixon's mind, the turning point was the first debate. "It was tough," he said. "I was the challenger, and he was the experienced incumbent. Once that debate was over, I was on my way to eventual victory."

In his memoirs Nixon strangely saw nothing wrong with linking Congressman Voorhis with the forces of the radical left even though the charge had no basis in fact. Later, Nixon even admitted as much when he said, "Of course I knew Jerry Voorhis wasn't a Communist. . . . The important thing is to win." He also claimed that "the greatest advantage I had in 1946 was that the national trend that year was Republican." In Nixon's rationale, "communism was not the central issue in the 1946 campaign" and "the PAC controversy provided emotional and rhetorical excitement, but it was not the issue that stirred or motivated most voters." For Richard Nixon, politics was war, and in war there are casualties. For the rest of his public life, truth was often to become a casualty of Richard Nixon's politics—a politics in which winning was everything.

Meanwhile, on the other side of the country in Massachusetts, a young Irish-Catholic patrician, John F. Kennedy, handily won his campaign for Congress. Kennedy and Nixon would enter the freshman congressional class of 1947 together and although they started out as friends, a rivalry would ensue that would only be quelled by the fierce presidential face-off in 1960.

3

NIXON IN THE NATIONAL ARENA
From Congress to the Senate

> "I'm telling you fellows, one of these days you fellows right here will be guests in the White House. . . . I won't be here when the time comes, but you fellows right here will be guests of Dick Nixon's in the White House some day."
>
> —H. L. Perry

When Richard Nixon entered the House of Representatives in 1947, the Republican Party was in control of the House for the first time since 1931. The party was determined not to squander the fruits of its hard-won victory and looked toward the presidential election of 1948 to finally end the long reign the Democrats had enjoyed under Franklin D. Roosevelt's New Deal and Harry Truman's Fair Deal.

For the most part, new congressmen do their best to remain in the background as they pay close attention to the constituents who elected them and learn the ins and outs of Washington's fast-paced political and social whirl. As historian Stephen E. Ambrose writes in *Nixon: The Education of a Politician*, "Freshmen congressmen are supposed to be seen and not heard, but the unique circumstances of the Eightieth Congress gave Nixon an opportunity to play a leading role in three major areas—labor reform, subversive control, and foreign aid. He seized his opportunity so effectively that by the end of the session he was widely recognized as a comer."

The Nixons moved to Washington after the Christmas holidays, and on January 3, 1947, Nixon was sworn in as a congressman. A reporter asked the ambitious new lawmaker if he had any special goals or legislation in mind. "No, nothing in particular," Nixon answered. But after a moment of thought Nixon added, "I was elected to smash the labor bosses." As a result, the new Speaker of the House, Joe Martin, already alerted by Nixon mentor Herman L. Perry to be on the lookout for the promising new California congressman, saw to it that Nixon received two plum committee assignments. Because of his stated hostility toward organized labor Nixon was appointed to the Education and Labor Committee. His second committee assignment, to the House Committee on Un-American Activities (known as HUAC), came at a time when the cold war between the United States and the Soviet Union was beginning and it ultimately thrust Nixon onto center stage of the nation's political life. Thus, from the very beginning, Nixon seemed destined to play a major role in postwar American life.

Although the United States and the Soviet Union had been allies during World War II, in the postwar world Americans began to distrust the Soviets and their murderous leader Joseph Stalin. Like Vladimir Lenin, the architect of the 1917 Russian Revolution, Stalin had brutally consolidated his power by murdering his opponents or exiling them for life in a network of harsh labor camps known as the gulag. Communism, the ideology that supposedly drove the Soviet economic engine, had turned out to be a brutal and oppressive system that some political theorists actually compared with Nazism. With its heartless suppression of individual and human rights, its antireligious bias, and its steadfast opposition to the West and capitalism, the Soviet Union was seen as a major threat to world peace by many in the West. Winston Churchill, the stalwart British prime minister whose resolution and bravery had led the English through the darkest years of World War II, had declared that an "Iron Curtain" had fallen across Europe in 1945 when the Soviets had occupied Poland, Czechoslovakia, Latvia, Lithuania, Hungary, and eastern Germany, among other regions.

With the onset of the cold war, it was inevitable that anticommunism, which had been simmering before the war, would move to the front burner of American politics. The House Committee on Un-American Activities became one of the launching pads for ambitious politicians seeking to grab the spotlight of national notoriety by hunting for Communists and other "subversives" in American public life. The new Republican Speaker of the House, Joe Martin, had pledged to cooperate with HUAC and to "remove the Red Menace from America."

In his memoirs Nixon tells us that his HUAC appointment "was an offer I could not very well refuse. I accepted with considerable reluctance . . . because of the dubious reputation the committee had acquired." The truth is that Nixon was gleeful over the appointment, which made him the only California congressman to sit on two powerful and very visible House committees. As one Washington journalist, Roger Morris, wrote, "Such a plum could only mean that powerful influence had been exerted on his behalf."

For a young and unknown congressman with the ambition to make a national name and reputation for himself quickly, the anticommunist sentiment that was sweeping the United States in the late 1940s provided the ideal setting. For Richard Nixon it became a godsend.

A colleague on the Labor Committee, the Wisconsin freshman Republican Charles Kersten, had been deeply involved in the investigation of Communist influence in the American labor movement. Kersten introduced Nixon to Father John F. Cronin, a professor at St. Mary's Seminary in Baltimore. Father Cronin had been active in the labor movement and had become alarmed at the extent of Communist influence in American labor. Although Father Cronin was hardly typical of the red-baiters who followed him and had actually devoted much of his life to the cause of social justice, he had taken time off from teaching in order to study the labor movement and had begun to gather data on Communist infiltration of organized labor. Father Cronin's study, "The Problem of American Communism," included an FBI report with testimony by Whittaker Chambers, an ex-Communist who was then a senior editor of *Time* magazine. Chambers had named names, exposing alleged Communists.

Father Cronin was greatly disturbed at what he found. He was especially concerned that high-level government officials were apparently indifferent to his findings. Father Cronin met with Nixon on at least four occasions in Baltimore in early 1947. Cronin urged Nixon to read his material and put him in touch with a number of ex-Communists. He apparently convinced Nixon that there were Communists working in the State Department.

It must be recalled that anticommunism, so prevalent in the late 1940s, was not confined to the Republican Party. Democratic president Harry Truman had acted decisively to stop the spread of communism in Greece and Turkey by pouring financial aid into those countries. Truman's foreign policy, which became known as "containment," had the goal of confining communism to the eastern European nations that had become satellites within the Soviet orbit.

In July 1947, President Truman invited small groups of Republican congressmen to the White House, where he explained his international objectives in an effort to gain bipartisan support for his foreign policy. Congressman Nixon, undoubtedly impressed with the fact that he had been called in to meet with the president of the United States, felt that Truman's policy made good sense. Nixon gladly jumped on the anticommunist bandwagon although, according to Stephen E. Ambrose, "Nixon was more concerned with exposing Communists at home than he was with fighting them abroad."

Nixon's opportunity came on August 3, 1948, when Whittaker Chambers was called to testify before HUAC on the subject of Communist infiltration of the federal government. Chambers told the committee how he had become a member of the Communist Party in 1924 and related his growing disenchantment with the party in the 1930s. He then revealed that he had belonged to a group of Communists whose aim had been to infiltrate the American government. According to Nixon,

> Chambers was a man of extraordinary intellectual gifts and one who had inner strength and depth. Here was no headline-seeker but rather a thoughtful, introspective

man, careful with his words, speaking with what sounded like the ring of truth.

Among the four men named as Communists in this group was Alger Hiss. A graduate of Harvard Law School, Hiss had served as an aide to Supreme Court Justice Oliver Wendell Holmes, as an assistant secretary of state in the Roosevelt administration, and then as secretary-general of the San Francisco Conference, where the Charter of the United Nations was drafted. In 1947 Hiss had left the government to become president of the prestigious Carnegie Endowment for International Peace.

Clearly, the charges against Hiss were potentially explosive. Could someone with Hiss's elite background and credentials actually have been part of a sinister conspiracy to penetrate the highest circles of American government? More important, how could a member of the outlawed Communist Party, dedicated to the overthrow of American democracy, reach such high levels of government? Nixon instinctively understood that many Americans might well be deeply troubled by such questions.

Hiss immediately went on the offensive. The next day he sent a telegram to the committee requesting the opportunity to testify. Hiss was invited to appear on August 5. The tall, handsome, and aristocratic Hiss was a striking contrast to the disheveled, sweaty, and portly Chambers as he categorically denied the charges in a clear, firm voice:

> I am here at my own request to deny unqualifiedly various statements about me which were made before this committee by one Whittaker Chambers the day before yesterday. I am not and have never been a member of any Communist front organization. I have never followed the Communist Party line, directly or indirectly. To the best of my knowledge none of my friends is a Communist.

As one reporter later noted, "When Hiss concluded his testimony, the general feeling in Washington was that the long-controversial Un-American Activities Committee had made its final blunder, and was finished. Hiss had impressed practically everyone with the implication that the committee had been duped into permitting Chambers to use it as a forum from which to slander people." One congressman, the old Mississippi Democrat John Rankin, was so moved that he rose from his seat to shake Hiss's hand. Even President Truman decried the Republican attempts to hold "spy hearings" as "a red herring to keep from doing what they ought to do" about the nation's other pressing problems.

After Hiss testified, the committee went into secret session in, as Nixon described it, "a virtual state of shock." One Republican member complained, "We've been had. We're ruined." Only Nixon seemed to remain suspicious. As he later said, "Hiss was much too smooth . . . much too careful a witness for one who purported to be telling the whole truth without qualifications. . . . I felt he had put on a show when he was shown a picture of Chambers."

Nixon was able to convince his colleagues to allow him to chair a subcommittee to question Chambers again in executive session without the presence of the press or the public. Nixon was fully aware of the gravity of the situation. If Hiss was innocent, the person who continued to pursue the issue could have little hope of a political future. As Nixon later recalled in his book *Six Crises,*

> I had a natural sense of achievement over my success in preventing the Committee from dropping the case prematurely. . . . I had put myself, a freshman Congressman, in the position of defending the reputation of the Un-American Activities Committee. And in so doing, I was opposing the President of the United States and the majority of press corps opinion, which is so important to the career of anyone in elective office. Also, my stand, which was based on my own opinion and judgment, placed me more or less in the corner of a former Communist functionary and against one of the brightest, most respected young men following a public career. Yet I could not go against my own conscience and my conscience told me that, in this case, the rather unsavory-looking Chambers was telling the truth, and the honest-looking Hiss was lying.

Nixon's reasons for pushing on have been the subject of intense speculation. According to scholar Allen Weinstein, Nixon had seen advance information about Hiss in government security files (information not made available to the others on the committee) and had possibly been briefed on Hiss by Father Cronin. Also, according to Weinstein, Nixon had developed "an intense personal dislike of Alger Hiss."

The committee's chief investigator, Robert Stripling, also believed that Hiss was lying. But Stripling was also convinced that there was a deep-rooted animosity between Nixon and Hiss. Stripling said, "Nixon had his hat set for Hiss. . . . It was a personal thing. He was no more concerned about whether or not Hiss was [a Communist] than a billy goat!"

Weinstein is supported by psychohistorian Bruce Mazlish, who writes, "Alger Hiss . . . was everything Nixon was not. . . . Hiss, the embodiment of Eastern values, treated Nixon, the thirty-five-year-old freshman congressman, like dirt." At one point in their exchange Hiss is alleged to have goaded Nixon by saying, "I graduated from Harvard. I heard your school was Whittier." Apart from his dislike of Hiss, Nixon's decision to press the case might well have stemmed from the sincere and deeply held belief that Hiss was not only a liar but a Communist spy who had betrayed his country. As Stephen E. Ambrose has written, "That it took courage for Nixon to hold to his hunch cannot be doubted."

The plot in the Hiss-Chambers case took more bizarre twists and turns than most of the film noir detective mysteries or cheap dime-store pulp fiction of that era, and the case has gone down as one of the most complex criminal spy sagas of the 20th century. On December 15, 1948, after months of hearings and continued investigation, Alger Hiss was indicted by a federal grand jury for perjury for denying that he had ever turned over State Department documents to Whittaker Chambers. The first trial took five weeks and ended in an 8-to-4 deadlock. The second trial began on November 17, 1949, and on January 21, 1950, Hiss was found guilty. He served three years and eight months and was released in 1954. Maintaining his innocence up to the day of his death in 1996, Hiss drifted off into a life of obscurity, becoming a footnote in the history of the cold war and the rising political career of Richard M. Nixon.

For the purposes of Richard Nixon's upward political mobility, the Hiss case could not have come at a more opportune moment. When President Truman and his secretary of state, Dean Acheson, mistakenly came to Hiss's defense at the outset of the affair, many Americans began to wonder whether or not the Democrats actually did have a soft spot for the Communists. American anxiety about communism heightened in September 1949, when the Soviets exploded their first atomic bomb and the Chinese Communists expelled General Chiang Kai-shek's U.S.-supported Nationalists and proclaimed the People's Republic of China under Mao Tse-tung. The Democrats, who had just barely held on to the White House under Harry Truman in 1948, were now forced to defend themselves against charges that they were not tough enough on communism.

Nixon was in a perfect position to exploit this mood. Because of the Hiss case, everyone knew that he was tough on the Communists. In the ensuing political battles that Nixon fought in the late 1940s and early 1950s, he would charge on several occasions that a vote for the Democratic Party would yield "more Alger Hisses, more atomic spies, more crises."

With the Hiss case behind him, Richard Nixon put his powerful political ambition into high gear. When Democratic senator Sheridan Downey dropped out of the California primary because of poor health, California Republicans chose Nixon to oppose Democratic congresswoman Helen Gahagan Douglas for the vacant Senate seat. As William Costello wrote, "The 1950 contest (between Helen Gahagan Douglas and Nixon) was in all respects a Chotiner-Nixon tour de force, testing and refining their virtuosity and resourcefulness."

The Nixon-Douglas campaign started out as a close race. In the primary, Nixon had polled around a million votes and Helen Douglas, a former Broadway actress who was married to the well-known Hollywood actor Melvyn Douglas, had received around 890,000 votes. But once again the tides of history seemed to coincide with Nixon's rising political star. Three weeks after the primary, in June 1950, U.S. troops engaged Communist forces in Korea, ensuring that most Americans would continue to be preoccupied with the menace of communism.

The "red scare" was exactly what Nixon needed. He saw his opportunity and he took it. Thus, the Nixon campaign was dominated, as in the Voorhis race, by Nixon's growing inability to tell the truth—or at least the exact truth. Nixon's campaign literature, sent out to registered Democrats, was captioned with the words "As one Democrat to Another. . . ." While he never identified himself as a Republican in the pamphlet, Nixon made certain that every Democratic voter knew he was a family man, "a war hero," and of his central role in the famous Hiss case.

Nixon also found he could say one thing and do another. When he began his campaign against Congresswoman Douglas, Nixon was acutely aware of the fact that his opponent was a woman. Until recent times, the United States Senate, traditionally a bastion of male dominance, was difficult if not impossible for women to penetrate. Thus, Nixon would go out of his way to say, "I am confronted with an unusual situation. My opponent is a woman. . . . There will be no name-calling, no smears, no misrepresentation in this campaign." And then, Richard Nixon proceeded to do exactly that.

One scholar is convinced that Richard Nixon simply didn't like women. As Fawn M. Brodie writes, "Not only was Nixon contemptuous of women's intellect generally, but he was also oblivious to women as individuals." And Pat Nixon, who was hardly as silent as most observers of that time thought, once said, "I can hardly recall his paying a woman a compliment, except to remark on her hat."

In his campaign against Helen Gahagan Douglas, Nixon joined forces with Senator Joseph McCarthy of Wisconsin, who endorsed Nixon's crusade against Communists in high government circles. Both Nixon and McCarthy had called for the resignation of Truman's secretary of state, Dean Acheson. In fact, McCarthy actually joined a Nixon rally in California and charged Acheson with the high crime of treason, calling the Democrats under Truman "the administration Commicrat Party of Betrayal." Instead of denouncing McCarthy's ugly remarks, Nixon was silent.

To win the election, Chotiner and Nixon both felt that it was necessary to paint Douglas into a political corner by insinuating that she herself was sympathetic with communism. On August 20, 1950, the Nixon campaign published a broadside printed on pink paper (to show that Douglas was a little bit red) that stated in part:

> During five years in Congress, Helen Douglas has voted 353 times exactly as has Vito Marcantonio, the notorious

Communist party-line Congressman from New York. . . . How can Helen Douglas, capable actress that she is, take up so strange a role as a foe of communism? And why does she when she has so deservedly earned the title of "the pink lady"? . . . To the Communist newspaper *The New York Daily Worker*, Helen Douglas and Vito Marcantonio are heroes.

This became the famous "pink sheet" that claimed Douglas had voted with Marcantonio 354 times (the figure was upped by one) and in the next edition that Nixon had voted "the opposite to the Douglas-Marcantonio axis." Over a half million copies were then distributed. Although the charge was technically accurate, what Nixon failed to tell California voters was the very salient fact that most of those votes were inconsequential and hardly vital to the life of the republic. Furthermore, Nixon himself had voted with Marcantonio 112 times—another fact Nixon conveniently neglected to tell the voters.

The truth was that Douglas had supported the Marshall Plan, which had poured U.S. money into the European nations whose economies were most devastated by World War II. This bold and forward-looking policy had certainly helped to stem the tide of communism. In addition, Douglas had voted for a number of Truman measures that were clearly anticommunist and anti-Soviet in their intent. To charge, as Nixon did, that Douglas had "consistently supported the State Department's policy of appeasing communism in Asia which finally resulted in the Korean War" was patently ridiculous.

But the charges stuck, and events continued to go Nixon's way as well. In the last days of the race, the conflict in Korea escalated when six divisions of the Chinese Communist army crossed the Yalu River into Korea and overran the American forces, delivering a crushing blow to American morale at home and abroad. The Douglas campaign made a number of halfhearted attempts to counter Nixon's scurrilous charges and also made the fatal mistake of distorting Nixon's own record—a mistake the Nixon troops gleefully refuted, with the cooperation of the press. Despite his lifelong battle with the press, in 1950 Nixon could have no complaints about its treatment of him. Of twelve California newspapers, nine supported Nixon, two supported Douglas, and one was neutral—representing a circulation of six to one in Nixon's favor. The influential *Los Angeles Times* called Nixon "the most conspicuous opponent of communism in Congress" and put Douglas down as a "glamorous actress, who though not a Communist, voted the Communist line in Congress innumerable times." The widely circulated paper went on to vilify Douglas as "the darling of the Hollywood parlor pinks and Reds."

The final vote was 2,183,454 for Nixon, 1,502,507 for Douglas. In one of the nastiest Senate races in California history, Richard Nixon had put an end to the political career of Helen Douglas. After a brief return to the stage, she ended her public life altogether. But she did manage to leave the American people one lasting legacy. In an angry editorial, a California newspaper named the *Independent Review* condemned the ugly defamation of Douglas, noting that "representatives of her senatorial opponent, Tricky Dick Nixon, are the chief mouthpieces for this partisan effort to crucify Mrs. Douglas." The epithet "Tricky Dick" would be a millstone around Nixon's neck for the rest of his political life.

In 1957, Nixon apologized for his campaign against Douglas, telling *The New Republic*, "I'm sorry about that episode. I was a very young man." Years later, when he wrote his own memoirs, Nixon apparently had second thoughts:

> Helen Douglas lost the election because the voters of California in 1950 were not prepared to elect as their senator anyone with a left-wing voting record or anyone they perceived as being soft or naive about communism. She may have been at some political disadvantage because she was a woman. But her fatal disadvantage lay in her record and in her views.

Whatever Nixon really felt about the election of 1950, his victory had one indisputable result: the Republican Party, which had narrowly lost the 1948 presidential election, was already gearing up for 1952. The Republicans were expected to choose the aging World War II hero Dwight David Eisenhower as their presidential candidate; if they did, a popular young senator from a key electoral state like California might be just the thing they needed to balance the ticket.

As Stephen E. Ambrose wrote,

The Hiss case had made [Nixon] a national figure; the 1950 election made him a member of the nation's most exclusive club, and not just a member, but the senator who had won his seat with the largest margin of any senator elected or re-elected that year. His reputation among the big men in his party could hardly have been higher.

Within the short space of five years the young man from a humble California background had gotten himself elected to Congress and the United States Senate. Now Richard Nixon was positioned for serious consideration for the vice presidency of the United States.

4
FROM SENATOR TO VEEP

"... we did get something—a gift—after the election. ... It was a little cocker spaniel dog in a crate that he sent all the way from Texas. Black and white spotted. And our little girl—Tricia, the six-year-old—named it Checkers. And you know the kids ... love that dog and I just want to say this right now, that regardless of what they say about it, we're going to keep it."

—"The Checkers Speech" September 22, 1952

As the Republican Party looked toward the presidential election of 1952, they saw clear indications that the voters were growing restless after almost two decades of Democratic leadership. In the 1950 congressional elections the Republicans had gained five seats in the Senate and 28 in the House. As the party strategists began to lay the groundwork for victory in 1952 they could not fail to notice that the freshman senator from California had quickly become a Republican superstar. Richard Nixon was one of the most popular after-dinner speakers in the country. He managed, even with a very busy Senate schedule, to squeeze in at least a dozen speaking engagements a month as he traveled the United States to spread the new Republican gospel.

At the National Young Republic Convention in Boston on June 28, 1951, in an address Nixon called "The Challenge of

1952," he told the enraptured young Republicans that "the American people have had enough of the whining, whimpering, groveling attitude of our diplomatic representatives who talk of America's weaknesses and of America's fears rather than of America's strength and of America's courage." Harping on the spreading fear of communism, Nixon charged the Democrats under Truman with "failure . . . to develop an effective program to meet the activities of the fifth column [Soviet spies] in the United States." What had worked so well in California, Nixon believed, would be just as effective on the national scene. "Communists," Nixon charged, "infiltrated the very highest councils of this administration . . . our top administration officials have refused time and time again to recognize the existence of the fifth column in this country and to take effective action to clean subversives out of the administrative branch of our government."

As the Republican lines were drawn for the presidential election of 1952, it became increasingly apparent that the battle for the nomination would be between two men: Senator Robert A. Taft of Ohio and General Dwight D. Eisenhower. Taft, the son of a former president, had been in the Senate since 1939 and was known as "Mr. Republican." He was clearly the choice of the party establishment.

Dwight D. Eisenhower had served as supreme commander of the Allied forces in Europe during World War II and was the guiding strategic genius behind the famous D-Day invasion of June 6, 1944—the Allied landing at Normandy, France, that turned the tide of the war. He then served as army chief of staff and, in 1948, was named president of Columbia University. In 1950, Eisenhower returned to active military service as supreme commander of the North Atlantic Treaty Organization (NATO).

As the Republican convention neared, the first to approach Nixon with the idea of the vice presidency was the defeated Republican presidential candidate of 1948, Governor Thomas E. Dewey of New York. As Dewey's former campaign manager, Herbert Brownell, Jr., later recalled,

> Nixon seemed an almost ideal candidate for Vice-President. He was young, geographically right, had experience both in the House and the Senate with a good voting record, and was an excellent speaker.

On May 8, 1952, Dewey invited Nixon to be the keynote speaker at the New York State Republican Party's annual fund-raising dinner at the Waldorf Astoria Hotel. It was no secret that Dewey was a strong Eisenhower supporter and was working closely with Brownell on Eisenhower's behalf. After the speech Dewey invited Nixon to his hotel for a chat. According to Dewey, "The two of us sat around for about an hour and a half before he took his train. That was the occasion on which I discussed with him briefly the possibility of him becoming the Vice-President." With the nominating convention still two months off, Nixon couldn't believe Dewey was serious. But Nixon could hardly have been all that surprised. After all, he had been traveling throughout the country to get the attention of prominent Republicans from the time he was first elected to the Senate.

By the spring of 1952 many newspapers had gotten wind of what was going on behind the scenes and were prematurely suggesting the possibility of an "Ike-Dick" national ticket. Pat Nixon was hesitant—she didn't want to be burdened with yet another political campaign—but her husband seemed to be getting all his political ducks in a row for a serious run at the nomination.

Eisenhower himself was not certain about his running mate (he actually thought the choice was up to the convention). The field looked open to any one of a number of prominent Republicans. But at a meeting of Republican leaders, Governor Dewey spoke up strongly in behalf of Nixon, explaining all the benefits of having him on the ticket. As Herbert Brownell recalled, "by the time Dewey had finished everyone seemed to be convinced that Nixon was the right choice. There wasn't a lot of discussion after that. I called for a show of hands and it was unanimous. I reported to Eisenhower and he immediately gave his OK. That was it."

From George Washington's time on, the vice presidency of the United States had rarely been a coveted office. Even though many vice presidents (John Adams, Martin Van Buren, Andrew Johnson, Theodore Roosevelt, and Harry Truman, for example) have become president, the job up until Nixon's time was largely ceremonial and most vice presidents in American history have found little substance attached to the duties of their office. As Nixon himself said,

> The vice presidency had traditionally been a political dead end.... before 1952 it was more often a stepping-stone to political oblivion.... If I had had presidential ambitions—which I did not at that point—I probably would not have considered becoming Vice President.

In early July, Eisenhower was nominated on the first ballot at the Republican convention in Chicago, and the convention then turned to the business of selecting a vice president. Late in the evening, on the day of Eisenhower's nomination, Nixon was awakened by Herbert Brownell, who stated quite simply, "We picked you." Nixon dressed hurriedly, and the ever-resourceful Chotiner commandeered a limousine with a police escort to shuttle Nixon across the city to Eisenhower's hotel. Eisenhower, who hardly knew Nixon, welcomed him and told the ecstatic young California senator,

> Dick, I don't want a Vice President who will be a figurehead. I want a man who will be a member of the team. And I want him to be able to step into the presidency smoothly in case anything happens to me.

At the outset of the campaign Nixon was given the unenviable task of becoming Eisenhower's attack dog—the official "hit man" of the party. The Republican strategy was for Eisenhower to take the high road by emphasizing the positive. In the meantime, his running mate would take the low road. On the day after his nomination Nixon hit the campaign trail with all cylinders on full throttle. He held a press conference, met with congressional leaders to coordinate the national Republican effort, and made a speech before the Republican National Committee. The issues of the 1952 campaign, Nixon told the Republican faithful, were "the Truman record" and "Communism at home and abroad."

On July 28, 1952, the Whittier community responded to their hometown hero's success by welcoming Nixon back to the campus of his alma mater, Whittier College. A week later Governor Earl Warren of California told a Republican gathering that Nixon's nomination "is like a breath of fresh air to this country, and I believe the people will respond to it."

But there were dark clouds on Nixon's bright political horizon. For although it was unknown to Eisenhower and the horde of Republicans who were more than eager to climb on the Nixon bandwagon, Richard Nixon's California supporters had maintained an $18,000 political slush fund (an illegal campaign account) for him. Though this did not amount to much (by contemporary standards), it soon posed a political problem that almost sank Nixon's political ship before it ever got under way.

The "Nixon fund" was begun innocently enough. Nixon would be up for reelection to the Senate in 1956, and the fund would enable him to campaign continuously for reelection without waiting for Republican Party help. Nixon's backers, of course, had no idea that their candidate would be nominated for the vice presidency in 1952. Once he got the nomination, and once he began hammering away at the Democrats on the question of ethics and morality in government, it was only a matter of time before the fund became a major issue. After all, Eisenhower himself had said, "When we are through, the experts in shady and shoddy government operations will be on their way back to the shadowy haunts in the subcellars of American politics from which they came."

On September 18, 1952, the *New York Post,* a newspaper supporting the Democratic presidential candidate, former Illinois governor Adlai E. Stevenson, published the first anti-Nixon salvo with a bold full-page headline: "SECRET NIXON FUND."

At first the story seemed to have no legs. But when the chairman of the Democratic National Committee, Stephen Mitchell, called for Nixon to resign from the campaign, it became increasingly clear that Nixon would have to respond. Nixon's initial response was tepid. In what became his standard response to critics, Nixon refused to shoulder any blame and said,

> After the very difficult 1950 campaign, the people who had been active—my finance committee as well as others—sat down with me and said: "We want you to start campaigning right now for 1956, and we think that the way to do it is to have available the funds to make speeches, make trips to California and so forth." . . . The idea of a year-around campaign fund was theirs.

At a time when his Senate salary was $12,500 (in addition to $2,500 tax free for general expenses; $2,000 for telephone, telegraph, and stationery; $70,000 for staff; and one round-trip home per session) many Americans were angered when they heard of the Nixon fund. After all, people who worked hard for a living didn't have anyone raising tax-free "secret" funds for their personal enjoyment. Few Americans would be very sympathetic with any politician who spent $4,237.54 on Christmas cards alone in his first year in office (not to mention the thousands spent crisscrossing the United States to make an endless number of political speeches).

As the criticism escalated, Nixon continued to try to tough it out. "This is," he claimed, "another typical smear by the same left-wing elements which have fought me ever since I took part in the investigation which led to the conviction of Alger Hiss." But it was hardly the political left, or even the Democrats, that were most vocal. Within a matter of days Nixon's candidacy was under assault from members of his own party. Now Nixon was in deep trouble. The *New York Herald Tribune*, a powerful Republican newspaper, called on Nixon to withdraw from the campaign. The *New York Times*, which had been supporting Eisenhower, editorialized that the men who gave money to Nixon "showed poor judgment in making such a gift and Senator Nixon had shown poor judgment in accepting it." A national survey of almost 100 newspapers, the majority of which supported the Republicans, now disapproved of Nixon by a ratio of two to one.

In the beginning Eisenhower did his best to put some distance between himself and his now-besieged running mate. When the Eisenhower campaign train was traveling through Iowa and Nebraska, all Eisenhower's press secretary, James Hagerty, would say was "We never comment on a *New York Post* story." But the press smelled a big story and tried its best to move it along. On Eisenhower's campaign train reporters voted 40 to 2 against Nixon's chances of staying on the ticket and claimed that the Republicans were preparing a "whitewash" of the Nixon fund story. This prompted an angry retort from Eisenhower: "I don't care if you fellows are forty-to-two against me, but I'm taking my time on this. Nothing's decided, contrary to your idea that this is all a setup for a whitewash of Nixon. Nixon has got to be as clean as a hound's tooth."

Privately, however, Eisenhower was appalled. Other prominent Republicans, including Brownell, Dewey, and Harold Stassen, tried to distance themselves from Nixon. Stassen even sent Nixon a model resignation letter. But Nixon, convinced he had done nothing wrong, repeatedly denied that he gave out any favors to any of the individuals who had contributed to his fund.

Everyone in Washington was well aware that a number of congressional leaders had developed the practice of maintaining slush funds. But Nixon was his party's candidate for the second most powerful office in American government and it was inevitable, once the fund story got out, that his candidacy would be in deep trouble. As Fawn M. Brodie writes, "Nixon had been caught like the lust-abhorring pastor found petting in the choir loft."

While Nixon put on his best public face, he was privately humiliated and deeply hurt by what appeared to be Eisenhower's reluctance to give him unqualified support. As Nixon later wrote of Eisenhower's caution, "I must admit that it made me feel like the little boy caught with jam on his face."

In Kansas, Eisenhower finally ended his silence by predicting that "the facts will show that Nixon would not compromise with what is right." Nixon was buoyed by Eisenhower's statement, but when Senator Fred Seaton telephoned Chotiner on Eisenhower's behalf, Nixon's spirits fell once again. Eisenhower apparently wanted to speak to Nixon directly, and he wanted to get to the bottom of the whole thing.

Now, under intense scrutiny by the media and with the pressure rapidly mounting for him to resign, Nixon was at the breaking point. Shortly before he gave a speech in Portland, Oregon, to the Temple Beth Israel Men's Club—Murray Chotiner later said, "For all we knew, it was going to be the last speech of the campaign for him"—Nixon received a telegram from his mother that caused him to break down weeping. The ever-supportive Hannah Nixon told her besieged son, "Girls [Nixon's daughters Julie and Tricia] are okay . . . we are thinking of you and everything will be fine."

Many advisers were now urging Eisenhower to drop Nixon from the ticket. It might well have happened if Nixon had not decided to take the matter out of Eisenhower's hands by making a broad appeal to the American people. Nixon recalled that Thomas E. Dewey was the one who advised, "I think you should go on television. . . . I don't think Eisenhower should make this decision."

On the evening of September 23, 1952, Nixon was scheduled to appear for a half-hour on national radio and television from a Los Angeles studio. The $75,000 fee for the time was paid by the Republican National Committee, and 55 million Americans either watched or listened to Richard Nixon make the most crucial speech of his brief political life.

Arriving at the studio, Nixon conquered a case of last-minute jitters. His voice broke as he told Pat he couldn't go on. "Of course you can," Pat responded calmly as she took his hand and walked onto the stage with her husband. Finally, seated behind a desk, Nixon addressed the American people:

> My fellow Americans, I come before you tonight as a candidate for the Vice-Presidency . . . and as a man whose honesty and integrity has been questioned. . . . I am sure that you have read the charge and you've heard it that I, Senator Nixon, took $18,000 from a group of my supporters.

Nixon's speech was a gamble, alternately designed to deal with the charges that had been leveled against him and to tug at the emotions of the American public. Whatever Eisenhower might have planned to do about his running mate was checked and then checkmated again in what became known as "the Checkers speech." Nixon argued that none of the money in the $18,000 special fund had benefited him or his family personally. The funds, he maintained, were all used for "one message, of exposing this Administration, the Communism in it, the corruption in it." But, for the most part, Nixon spoke about growing up in modest circumstances and about his family. He told of his wartime service and of "the best thing that ever happened to me. I married Pat." Pat Nixon, he said, "doesn't have a mink coat. But she does have a respectable Republican cloth coat. And I always tell her that she'd look good in anything."

Midway through the speech Nixon used his children to tug at the heartstrings of his large television and radio audience. Telling of one gift he did accept, Nixon said,

> It was a little cocker spaniel dog in a crate that he sent all the way from Texas. Black and white spotted. And our little girl—Tricia, the six-year-old—named it Checkers. And you know the kids, like all kids, love that dog and I just want to say this right now, that regardless of what they say about it, we're going to keep it.

Having softened his audience up, Nixon then played his trump card. He would place his political fate in the hands of the American people:

> ... the decision [to stay on the ticket], my friends is not mine. I would do nothing that would harm the possibilities of Dwight Eisenhower to become President of the United States; and for that reason I am submitting to the Republican National Committee tonight, through this television broadcast, the decision which it is theirs to make. Let them decide whether my position on the ticket will help or hurt; and I am going to ask you to help them decide. Wire and write the Republican National Committee whether you think I should stay or whether I should get off; and whatever their decision is, I will abide by it.... Regardless of what happens, I am going to continue this fight.... And remember, folks, Eisenhower is a great man, believe me. He is a great man. And a vote for Eisenhower is a vote for what's good for America.

Dwight and Mamie Eisenhower watched Nixon's speech from the Cleveland Public Auditorium, where the general had been scheduled to speak at a campaign rally. At the end of Nixon's remarks Mrs. Eisenhower was weeping, and several of the Eisenhower aides were dabbing at their eyes with handkerchiefs. While the general himself carefully controlled his emotions, he could hear the audience in the auditorium below begin to chant, "We want Nixon! We want Nixon!" Turning to Arthur Summerfield, chairman of the Republican National Committee, Eisenhower said, "Well, Arthur, you certainly got your $75,000 worth tonight!" And Eisenhower's harried press secretary, James Hagerty, turned to his boss and said, "General, you'll have to throw your speech away. Those people out there want to hear about Nixon."

FROM SENATOR TO VEEP ■ 41

Richard and Pat Nixon campaigning in Boston (Boston Public Library)

As Eisenhower hastily scribbled notes for a new speech, Richard Nixon was busy apologizing to his wife, and to his friends Bill Rogers, Murray Chotiner, and Pat Hillings, for going over his allotted time and for forgetting to give the address of the Republican National Committee. But it didn't really matter. When the messages that came in to Republican Party headquarters in Washington alone were totaled, it was estimated that there were 300,000 letters, cards, telegrams, and petitions signed by over a million people. The support for Nixon was massive—almost 350 to one. And, to make Nixon look even better, money rolled in—mostly one-dollar contributions—to pay almost $60,000 toward the cost of the broadcast.

But to Nixon's great dismay, Eisenhower would not accept one speech as the solution to the Nixon political problem. That night Eisenhower sent Nixon a telegram summoning him to a face-to-face meeting in Wheeling, West Virginia:

> YOUR PRESENTATION WAS MAGNIFICENT. WHILE TECHNICALLY NO DECISION RESTS WITH ME, YOU AND I KNOW THE REALITIES OF THE SITUATION REQUIRE A PRONOUNCEMENT

WHICH THE PUBLIC CONSIDERS DECISIVE. MY PERSONAL DECISION IS GOING TO BE BASED ON PERSONAL CONCLUSIONS. I WOULD MOST APPRECIATE IT IF YOU CAN FLY TO SEE ME AT ONCE. TOMORROW I WILL BE AT WHEELING, W. VA. WHATEVER PERSONAL AFFECTION AND ADMIRATION I HAD FOR YOU—AND THEY ARE VERY GREAT—ARE UNDIMINISHED.

Nixon was livid. "What more can he possibly want from me?" he angrily asked Murray Chotiner. As Nixon told it, "I would not humiliate myself further by going to Wheeling." He called his secretary, Rose Mary Woods, into his hotel room and dictated a letter of resignation, instructing her to send it to Eisenhower immediately. Fortunately, Woods gave the typed resignation letter to Chotiner, who read it and then tore it up. Later, when he had calmed down, Nixon made arrangements to meet with Eisenhower in West Virginia.

As Eisenhower's campaign train rolled through the West Virginia countryside, the general hardly needed a pollster to tell him that the American public's sympathies were running heavily in favor of his running mate. Every time Eisenhower mentioned Nixon's name, the crowds shouted out their strong approval. Stacks of pro-Nixon telegrams were piled high on the train. The closer he got to Wheeling, the more Eisenhower warmed to the idea of keeping Nixon on the ticket. In fact, when Nixon's plane landed in Wheeling, Eisenhower was there to greet him personally. "General," an overwhelmed Nixon blurted out, "you didn't need to come out to the airport." "Why not?" Eisenhower responded with a wide trademark grin. "You're my boy!" Overcome with the powerful emotion of the moment, Nixon collapsed weeping into the arms of his old friend Senator William Knowland. After Eisenhower and Nixon spoke for about six minutes, the general ended the debate, saying, "He is not only completely vindicated as a man of honor but as far as I am concerned he stands higher than ever before."

The Democrats were outraged. How could Eisenhower have made up his mind about Nixon after a brief six-minute conversation? What about explaining the down payments Nixon had made on two homes in Washington and Whittier? What about the ethics of taking money that might influence the way a senator might vote on a given issue? None of these questions mattered. The Nixon fund question wasn't about ethics. It was about politics. Nixon had fooled them all. Even the press, which had always viewed Nixon with a jaundiced eye, grew misty in the wake of the Checkers speech. Robert Ruark, a tough veteran columnist with Scripps-Howard, was typical:

> Dick Nixon stripped himself naked for all the world to see, and he brought the missus and the kids and the dog and his war record into the act.... The sophisticates ... sneer ... [but] this came closer to humanizing the Republican party than anything that has happened in my memory.

Years later, Richard Bergholz, a retired reporter who had written for the *Los Angeles Times*, recalled the Checkers speech with a note mixing his skepticism with political realism:

> In my limited contact with Nixon, what I saw was a cold calculating man who treated Pat like just a piece of furniture in the hotel room.... If you read the transcript of what he really said in the "Checkers" speech, that was a hell of a tour de force; he did a great job. That was a tremendous ad lib presentation. Sure, it was a case when he talked about Checkers, and Pat's cloth coat, and he's really a poor guy. It wasn't the real Nixon. But it was right on the button.

Was it possible? Could Nixon have been as cold and calculating as some of his critics later charged? Was the Checkers speech contrived? Was Richard Nixon acting? Nixon himself provides us with an answer. On September 14, 1955, three years after the Checkers speech saved his political career, Nixon spoke at a luncheon given by the Radio and Television Executives Society. Perhaps he was more relaxed than usual. Whatever the reason, Nixon grinned at his audience and said, "You all remember the 'Checkers' speech I suppose." Those present chuckled as Nixon continued. "Well, I want you to be the first to know. . . ." Then Nixon paused for effect as the executives leaned forward in their seats to hear his next words. "I staged it," Nixon said. "There were times," Fawn M. Brodie noted, "when Nixon took an actor's satisfaction in the 'Checkers' speech."

The Checkers speech had resuscitated Nixon's political life. He stayed on the ticket and the Republican Party went on to win a landslide victory, with 39 states moving into the Republican column in 1952. At the age of 39 Richard M. Nixon had been elected vice president of the United States.

As historian Herbert S. Parmet astutely observed:

> The Checkers speech, as much as the Hiss affair, established Nixon as a political figure. The secret fund affair did something else . . . the speech itself found its way into the sympathies of the millions who could understand and wanted confirmation that Richard Nixon, although a Republican—the party of big business and Wall Street—shared their everyday anxieties, an altogether different audience from those who thought that the Checkers and Republican cloth coat stuff was "nauseating." Pat had found it hard to swallow. Nixon knew better.

As for Nixon himself, the price he would ultimately pay seemed imperceptible as Dwight Eisenhower and the Republicans prepared to take over the reins of power in 1953. Everything seemed to be coming up roses. What Nixon forgot is that all roses have thorns.

Once ensconced in the presidency, except for the times he was seriously ill, Eisenhower shunted Nixon aside. Nixon did the best he could under difficult and humiliating circumstances. Still, the next eight years must have been hard on him. Nixon became, in many respects, little more than an errand boy for the administration while never being admitted to the inner White House circles.

Nixon may have succeeded in going over Eisenhower's head during the campaign but he could hardly go over the head of the president, who became something of a father figure to him. Nixon complained to a reporter that "despite his [Eisenhower's] great capacity for friendliness, he also had a quality of reserve which, at least subconsciously, tended to make a visitor feel like a junior officer coming in to see the commanding General."

During the highly publicized 1954 Army-McCarthy hearings on national television, the Eisenhower administration sent Nixon out as its point man to counter the nation's leading anticommunist, the demagogic senator from Wisconsin, Joseph McCarthy. Eisenhower could hardly permit a liar and a redbaiter like McCarthy to outflank the administration, so Nixon was given the unenviable task of attack dog. It was a delicate job for Nixon, who had to persuade the American people that while the Republicans were four-square against communism, they would not reduce themselves to the gutter level of a Joe McCarthy, who had made increasingly reckless charges about alleged Communist influence in government and other profes-

Vice President Richard M. Nixon (Boston Public Library)

sions. Speaking publicly, Nixon agreed that the Communists were "a bunch of rats." But he made certain to tell his audience that "when you go out to shoot rats, you have to shoot straight, because when you shoot wildly it not only means that the rat may get away more easily, you make it easier on the rat, but you might hit someone else who's trying to shoot rats, too."

As vice president, Nixon worked very hard. He usually arrived by nine and seldom left before six. With a staff that was small compared with those of the top politicians of later eras, he managed to answer a very heavy volume of mail and give as many as three speeches a week, all of which he wrote himself. Nixon also took it upon himself to conduct seminars for newly elected Republicans, and his office was always open to state and local party officials who were visiting Washington. In addition, he sometimes presided over the Senate, sat in frequently on meetings of the cabinet and the National Security Council, and met often with Republican legislative leaders. With a small budget of just under $50,000, Nixon ran an effective operation. He read eight to ten newspapers every day and on weekends caught up with the weekly news periodicals.

Nixon's stock in the Eisenhower administration rose in the aftermath of the president's three serious illnesses between 1955 and 1957. In September of 1955 Nixon received a call from the president's press secretary. "Dick," he said, "this is Jim Hagerty—the president has had a coronary." Nixon later described his reaction in his book *Six Crises:*

> It is impossible to describe how I felt when I heard these words. The news was so unexpected, the shock so great that I could think of nothing to say for several seconds... . What I thought of, what concerned me, was not the awesome problems I would have if I should become President, but how I could best handle my immediate responsibility as a Vice President who was now, more than any of his thirty-five predecessors, "one heartbeat from the presidency." . . . How I reacted to this crisis was infinitely more important to the nation and the world than the way I handled the Hiss case or my fight to stay on the ticket in 1952.

Because at that time there was no clear constitutional rule dealing with the incapacity of a sitting president, Nixon's situation was both complex and politically dangerous. He was forced to balance himself on that thin line between appearing to be in control of events and appearing too ambitious for power. As he wrote, "There is a political axiom that where a vacuum exists, it will be filled by the nearest or strongest power. That had to be avoided at all costs." Nixon's task, as he put it, was to see to it that the Eisenhower team approach to governing continued to function as usual, and to avoid "any semblance of a struggle for dominance."

Nixon comported himself very well under what many observers agreed was immense strain and a most difficult situation. Although Eisenhower recovered within a matter of weeks, there was no question that he had almost died. At a meeting of the president's cabinet over which he presided, Nixon pointed out that the routine matters of governing the nation had to continue but that federal officials should not establish new policies in the absence of the president. Nixon also informed those present at the meeting that they should make every effort to remind the American people that they still represented the Eisenhower administration and that the government had not changed. As the members of the cabinet rose to adjourn, Secretary of State John Foster Dulles stated that the vice president had guided the government through a difficult period and was therefore entitled to an expression of the cabinet's appreciation. All those present applauded.

The Eisenhower-Nixon team was easily reelected in 1956, with the Democrats sending Adlai Stevenson once again to serve as their sacrificial lamb. The election was a landslide, with the Republicans carrying 41 states to Stevenson's seven and achieving an overwhelming popular vote of 35.6 million to 26 million. But although the election undoubtedly confirmed Eisenhower's popularity, the Republicans lost control of both houses of Congress. For the first time in 108 years, a president was elected without seeing his party carry either the House or the Senate.

In Eisenhower's second term Nixon was able to carve out a new role for himself. If Nixon had been an errand boy in the first term, the second term gave him a chance to develop his own interests and his own areas of expertise. With Eisenhower's approval, the vice president became a world traveler. Between 1957 and 1960, he met with numerous world leaders as a representative of the United States. His trips took him to the Far East, the Middle East, and the major capitals of Europe as well as to South America and the Soviet Union. These trips were not always pleasant. In Caracas, Venezuela, in 1958, the Nixon entourage was met by thousands of rock-throwing anti-American demonstrators chanting "Go Home Nixon!" and "Death to Nixon!" At his hotel Nixon was greeted by an angry protester who actually spit in his face. All of this was a big political plus for Nixon at home, where he was applauded for his courage. In his memoirs he recalled, "For the first time I pulled even with [John F.] Kennedy in the Gallup presidential trial heat polls."

Nixon's travels clearly opened his eyes to the intricacies and dangers of American foreign policy and diplomacy in a volatile postnuclear world. He quickly became an adept student of international affairs and an expert on foreign policy. Few in the government traveled as widely, met personally with as many world leaders, or learned as quickly on the job as Nixon. After Secretary of State John Foster Dulles died of cancer in 1959, no one in the president's inner circles knew as much about foreign policy as Nixon.

In 1959 Nixon visited the Soviet Union. In Moscow, he was able to engage Soviet premier Nikita Khrushchev in a series of highly publicized debates. Khrushchev, a fiercely outspoken Communist, called Nixon "a son of a bitch" and "an unprincipled puppet" of Joe McCarthy. Before his trip, Nixon trailed John F. Kennedy in the Gallup poll 61 percent to 39 percent. By November 1959 the gap had been overcome as Nixon pulled ahead of Kennedy, 53 percent to 47 percent. Nixon was now poised to make the move of his political life. Even Adlai Stevenson had to admit that Nixon's trips to Caracas and Moscow had made him "a formidable candidate" for the presidency in 1960.

5

NIXON VERSUS KENNEDY
The Election of 1960

"In 1960, I had suffered a shattering defeat in the Presidential campaign. It was no comfort that it was the closest election in history."

As Eisenhower's faithful vice president who had toiled long and hard in the Republican vineyards, Richard Nixon seemed to have the inside track on the Republican Party's nomination in 1960. Although his relationship with Eisenhower had never been particularly close, and Eisenhower had even seriously considered dropping Nixon from the ticket in 1956, Nixon had spent much of his time as vice president campaigning for Republican candidates every two years from 1954 to 1958. He had visited the small towns, villages, and posh suburbs that made up the core constituency of the Republican Party in every corner of the nation, and he knew almost every Republican ward boss and committeeman by name. As historian Herbert S. Parmet observed, "Nixon was the spark plug, energizing fellow Republicans, fighting to patch up intraparty divisions, and hailing the Administration for having saved America from 'Trumanism.'" The widely read and powerful Washington columnist Stewart Alsop wrote that Nixon best approximated Walter Lippmann's description of a "ruthless partisan."

Nixon had only one obstacle to overcome within the ranks of his own party: the liberal wing that was headed by New York's popular governor, Nelson A. Rockefeller. Rockefeller, the affable grandson and heir of Standard Oil tycoon John D. Rockefeller, stood out in stark contrast to Richard Nixon. As Garry Wills noted in *Nixon Agonistes,*

> True, Rockefeller was brought up in the same constrictive save-your-cash-and-your-soul religion that Nixon was. If anything, the pecuniary theologian John D. left a deeper mark on his whole brood than Whittier did on Nixon. The difference, of course, is that Nixon has spent his whole life on the way up—up a particularly jagged cliff. Nelson was born on top, king of the mountain, with only one moral duty, endlessly inculcated—to throw lifelines down to those stuck on the cliff. His means of self-improvement... is the offering of opportunity, not the seizing of it. He is the benevolent millionaire of the Alger stories, looking for ways to help the good boy up.

But Rockefeller, unlike Nixon, never really enjoyed the nuts and bolts of Republican Party organization. He rarely got down into the political trenches to attend the endless cold-chicken-and-peas dinners or to slug it out with the rank and file members of his party around the country. Rockefeller was just not well enough organized beyond New York State to constructively mount a serious stop-Nixon drive with the Republican faithful of the party.

It was no secret among Republicans that Rockefeller intensely disliked Nixon and considered him incapable of leading the American people. "I hate the thought of Dick Nixon being President of the United States," Rockefeller once told a close friend.

Nevertheless, Nixon had a firm grip on the large middle section of the Republican base. His eight years as vice president under the popular Eisenhower had served him well. He had amassed numerous friends and supporters. He had stacked up political markers that were owed to him from every corner of the nation. And Richard Nixon was the kind of politician who always made certain to collect on his political debts.

Nixon had kept his name in the headlines with his highly publicized travels to Europe and South America during his two-term vice presidency. And he may have impressed some Americans with his famous "kitchen debate" with Soviet leader Nikita Khrushchev during a 1959 visit to the American exhibit in Moscow.

In order for the Democrats to be successful in 1960 they would have to field a candidate who would ultimately be able to exploit Nixon's high negatives. Among the Democrats, the powerful and cunning Senate majority leader, Lyndon Baines Johnson of Texas, had a good chance to win the nomination. A party insider whose political roots went all the way back to Texas politics of the New Deal period, Johnson was supported by the influential Speaker of the House, Johnson's Texas mentor, Congressman Sam Rayburn. But Johnson had serious drawbacks. He was a southerner—and back in the 1960s southerners, along with Catholics, blacks, and Jews, were thought to be incapable of winning a national election. Moreover, Johnson seemed to represent the old Democratic Party that had been put together by Franklin D. Roosevelt in the New Deal coalition of the 1930s. These older Democrats were seen by the ambitious younger men as fossils—remnants of the Democratic Party of the past in which deals were made to distribute political power and patronage (jobs) by cigar-chomping political bosses in the smoke-filled back rooms of big-city hotels.

The clear front-runner for the new generation of Democrats was the handsome young senator from Massachusetts, John F. Kennedy. Kennedy, the wealthy son of a powerful Irish-Catholic family, had grown up in and around Boston in a life of style, privilege, and high expectations.

His father, Joseph P. Kennedy, had been President Roosevelt's ambassador to England before World War II. John Kennedy, like Nixon, had seen wartime service in the navy after being educated at exclusive private schools and graduating from Harvard. Kennedy had emerged from his war exploits as something of a national hero, with a little help from his father and his influential friends in the media.

In 1947 Kennedy arrived in Washington in the same freshman congressional class as Richard Nixon. At first, Nixon and Kennedy, whose congressional offices were across the hall from

John F. Kennedy and Richard M. Nixon (John F. Kennedy Library)

one another, got along very well and even played poker together. Nixon seemed to like the brash young New Englander, whose style and manner stood out in such stark contrast to his own more reserved personality and conduct. In 1955, when Kennedy was recovering from a life-threatening back operation in which he was given the last rites of the Catholic Church, he had received a huge basket of fruit from the vice president with a card that read, "Welcome home. Dick Nixon."

Kennedy and Nixon once even traveled together to McKeesport, Pennsylvania, to debate one another on the Taft-Hartley Act, a major piece of labor legislation. Since the bill restricted the rights of labor, Nixon was for it and Kennedy was against it. Sharing a sleeping car back to Washington late that evening, the two men stayed up most of the night discussing foreign policy. They discovered that, although they differed on many facets of domestic policy, they had both voted for Truman's foreign aid to Greece and Turkey, a measure that was designed to slow the growth of communism in those countries.

While Nixon had worked hard, risking the dangers of notoriety as a young congressman, Kennedy's congressional career was remarkably undistinguished even when he got to the Senate. Kennedy was known by most Washington insiders as a playboy and womanizer. Yet despite his differences from Nixon, their voting records, with a few minor exceptions, were similar.

As Herbert S. Parmet observed,

> Both men were representative of those who came to maturity right after the war. Inevitably, many were veterans eager to forget the recent past and participate in the great new era of high expectations. Whether in Massachusetts or California, their aspirations were similar. The differences lay in the sociological character of their rock-bottom support.

In the spring of 1960, Kennedy easily defeated Hubert Humphrey, his major rival for the presidential nomination, in two key Democratic primaries in Wisconsin and West Virginia. With his father's money, a highly charged young staff, and the attractive Kennedy family willing to crisscross the rural countryside and small towns, Kennedy was able to purchase more television time than Humphrey and knock him out of the race. The one possible stumbling block that Kennedy faced was the fact that he was a Roman Catholic. A Catholic had not run for the presidency since Governor Al Smith of New York was soundly defeated in 1928. The dean of presidential campaign journalists, Theodore H. White, writing in the wake of Kennedy's victory in Wisconsin, recalled, "Over and over again there was the handsome, open-faced candidate on the TV screen, showing himself, proving that a Catholic wears no horns."

At the Democratic convention, held during the first week of July in Los Angeles, the Kennedy forces were able to count 600 certain votes on the first ballot. With 700 votes needed for victory, and the danger that Kennedy's support would dissipate if the convention went to a second ballot, the Kennedy team swung into action. Commanded by ambitious young men like Robert Kennedy, Kennedy's younger brother and campaign manager, the Kennedy forces made use of vastly improved technology that allowed them to communicate orders instantly to aides on the floor of the convention. With the support of some major big-city bosses like Mayor Richard Daley of Chicago, the Kennedy troops marched to victory on the first ballot with 800 votes.

Kennedy accepted the nomination as some 35 million Americans watched the proceedings on television. Clearly, by 1960, politics had come into the living room of the average American family—a fact that was hardly lost on Kennedy. In his acceptance speech, he spoke in very general terms about the nation's problems, noting that "we stand today on the edge of a New Frontier—a frontier of unknown opportunities and perils—a frontier of unfulfilled hopes and threats."

Kennedy then surprised many observers when he chose Senate Majority Leader Lyndon Johnson as his vice presidential running mate. The two men had been bitter rivals in the spring primaries and did not really like one another very much. Robert Kennedy, especially, disliked Johnson, viewing him as a crude country bumpkin, and some labor leaders worried that the choice of Johnson, a southerner, would alienate black voters. However, the Kennedy strategy was wise. With Johnson on the ticket the Democrats now had two of the three major elements of the party on board: the South, and the urban bosses who actually led the rank and file of the party. The third element, labor, had no place else to go and would never support an antilabor Republican candidate like Richard Nixon anyway.

Nixon's major competitor, Nelson Rockefeller, had folded by December 1959 because of lack of support in the party, leaving the way open for Nixon to triumph in the Republican primaries.

To unite the party, Nixon leaked the idea of a vice presidential offer to Rockefeller, but Rockefeller rejected that notion, and he also turned down the chance to chair the Republican National Committee or keynote the upcoming Republican convention. That spring Rockefeller's faint presidential aspirations were revived. A planned summit meeting between President Eisenhower and Soviet premier Khrushchev was scuttled when an American U-2 spy plane on a mission for the Central Intelligence Agency (CIA) was shot down over Russia and the pilot, Gary Francis Powers, was taken into custody by the Soviets. The shaken American president denied any knowledge of the spying, but it was obvious to the Russians and the rest of the world that the United States had been caught and that Eisenhower was lying. With Khrushchev rattling his saber and Fidel Castro continuing to make trouble for the administration in Cuba, Rockefeller hoped that somehow the Republican Party would turn to him at the last minute for wisdom and guidance. Thus, he allowed one of his aides to put out the word that the New York governor would be available for a presidential draft at the nominating convention.

That August the Republicans gathered at their national convention in Chicago and, as expected, gave the nomination to Nixon, who was now closing in on the pinnacle of American politics at the relatively young age of 47. But despite his remarkable ascent, Nixon, who had entered politics to rise above the poverty of his early life, was still an unhappy and troubled man. As David Halberstam wrote, "In his own mind . . . he was a victim. He felt he had been badly treated both professionally and personally by Eisenhower and the men around him, consulted only when they needed him, otherwise kept in the servants' quarters. All this had sharpened his resentment." Even John F. Kennedy said, "Nixon is a nice fellow in private and a very able man. I worked with him on the Hill for a long time, but he seems to have a split personality; and he is very bad in public, and nobody likes him."

Nixon decided to run on the Eisenhower record of peace and prosperity. He would represent small-town America in all its hopes, dreams, and aspirations, because he was a man who had retained many of the same small-town virtues and prejudices himself. Even though Nixon was the candidate of big business, he had developed into the kind of American politician representative of the latter part of the 20th century: a man with few firmly grounded beliefs who would often bargain away what he truly felt if he thought it might get him a few more votes. Nixon would often take almost any position on an issue if he thought he could gain from it politically. More important, in the election year of 1960, Nixon was not a Catholic. While he himself would never bring up the issue of his rival's religion, he would hardly shrink from it if some of his supporters made subtle references to the links between Kennedy and Rome.

However (the religious issue aside), Nixon would make some fatal mistakes that would hurt him badly in the campaign. For one thing, he seemed to become more distant, more isolated, and more withdrawn from his staff. In his book *The Powers That Be*, journalist David Halberstam recorded the observations of those close to Nixon:

> Nixon was bitter about the past, bitter about Ike, openly contemptuous of Ike's political ability. . . . Nixon had changed in a decade from a reasonably approachable young man to a political megalomaniac. No one could tell him anything. He had decided that he was the ultimate politician.

To keep a wall between himself and the press he had come to despise, Nixon began to rely on the skills of a young advertising executive, H. R. (Bob) Haldeman. Their unique relationship, which was to last more than 13 years, increasingly cut Nixon off from the normal give-and-take of everyday argument and political debate he had mastered in Washington. One friend considered the Nixon-Haldeman matchup a tragic error because Nixon was so private and desperately shy and Haldeman so rigid, narrow, and unwilling to compromise. As another observer commented, "Nixon was by nature an excluder. Haldeman liked to exclude people. When Nixon's needs met Haldeman's abilities, you had an almost perfect formula for disaster." Or, as David Halberstam put it, "It was . . . like darkness reaching for darkness. Nixon so vulnerable to isolation, Haldeman so given to it."

Thus, Nixon, a man who rarely trusted many people to begin with, a politician used to controlling his affairs as a congressman, senator, and even as vice president, became in effect his own campaign manager.

A national campaign in the modern political era could hardly be managed with any ultimate success by the candidate himself. He would have enough to do dealing with the mentally and physically grueling demands of mastering the issues, delivering effective speeches, and making countless numbers of public appearances all over the country. Only a century before, after receiving the Republican nomination for president, Abraham Lincoln returned to his home in Illinois. It was then considered unseemly for a candidate to campaign for high public office. In 1960, with the birth of the modern high-tech presidential campaign, everything had changed. Nixon made the foolish mistake of promising to take his campaign to all 50 states and, in the attempt, literally wore himself out.

Nixon was so intent on doing everything himself that he even brushed aside an offer of help from Eisenhower. "Mister President," Nixon told Eisenhower, "I think you've done enough already." Eisenhower was initially miffed at Nixon and then became enraged. "Did you see him? Did you see him?" Eisenhower asked an aide, imitating Nixon hunched over with his shoulders bent. "Did you see that? When I had a front-line officer like that in World War II, I relieved him. He doesn't look like a winner to me." It was, perhaps, no accident that Eisenhower, when asked by reporters to list Nixon's accomplishments as his vice president, responded, "If you give me a few weeks, I'll think of some."

But Nixon's biggest mistake was to agree to an unprecedented series of nationally televised debates with Kennedy. These debates would alter the American political landscape and change political campaigning for the rest of the century.

Clearly, Nixon didn't understand where electronic journalism was heading by 1960. Forgetting the lessons of his masterful "Checkers" ploy, Nixon told writer Earl Mazo in 1959, "Television is not so effective as it was in 1952. The novelty has worn off."

Looking back, Nixon realized that the debates were a major tactical error. As he wrote in his memoirs,

> An incumbent seldom agrees willingly to debate his challenger, and I knew that the debates would benefit Kennedy more than me by giving his views national exposure, which

he needed more than I did. Further, he would have the tactical advantage of being on the offensive. As a member of Eisenhower's administration, I would have to defend the administration's record while trying to move the discussion to my own plans and programs. But there was no way I could refuse to debate without having Kennedy and the media turn my refusal into a central campaign issue. The question we faced was not whether to debate, but how to arrange the debates so as to give Kennedy the least possible advantage.

Nixon had been a champion debater in college, and he totally underestimated Kennedy's skills. Kennedy saw the debates as a chance to show himself off to the press and to the American people. He was surprised that Nixon had accepted his challenge, and said that Nixon was "a damn fool to agree to debate me on an equal-time TV basis. Just imagine if Eisenhower had had to do this against Stevenson in 1952 and 1956. He would have looked silly."

Kennedy prepared for the debates as if he were cramming for college finals. Two days before each debate, Kennedy's

Nixon and Kennedy debate on TV in 1960. (John F. Kennedy Library)

legislative assistant, Meyer "Mike" Feldman, would bring him a stack of briefing papers. On the day of the debate Feldman, Theodore Sorensen, and Richard Goodwin would spend hours rehearsing key points and concepts with Kennedy. Each night before he went to sleep Kennedy would scan three-by-five cards filled with facts and statistics that his team had carefully prepared. Kennedy would study thousands of pages dealing with Nixon's policies and views.

Unlike Kennedy, Nixon would spend his time preparing for the debates in virtual isolation. On the day before the first debate, exhausted from two weeks of nonstop campaigning, Nixon spent his prep time removed from his staff and alone with his wife. He had been hospitalized with an infected knee in the early weeks of September. As a result Nixon had lost weight and looked pale and gaunt. Nixon later admitted that not listening when he was advised to reduce his schedule was a mistake.

Why were the TV debates so important in 1960? In 1950 only 11 percent of American families owned a television set. By 1960 88 percent of Americans had a TV set. Thus, a candidate on TV in 1950 could hope to reach at most about 4,400,000 people. In 1960 that number had skyrocketed: by going on national television a politician could expect to reach at least 10 times that number.

The four debates were scattered throughout the fall: September 26 in Chicago; October 7 in Washington; October 13 in New York; and October 21 again in New York. All three networks—ABC, CBS, and NBC—participated. And when the debates were over, the network executives were amazed. Each broadcast had averaged an audience of between 65 and 70 million viewers.

The first debate in Chicago turned out to be the most important because it set the tone for those that followed. The visual contrast on TV between the two men was powerful. Kennedy appeared calm and confident. He projected an image of youth and manly vigor. His was the ideal style for the red-hot medium: cool.

Nixon, still recovering from his knee surgery, appeared tired and tense, and at times he even looked frightened on television. He had stubbornly refused any makeup, and because he had a dark complexion to begin with, looked as if he had forgotten to shave. As Nixon later recalled, "I was weak physically and appeared that way on television, in contrast to Jack Kennedy, who looked tan, rested, and in vigorous good health." Nixon ignored his key audience; instead, he directed his full attention to Kennedy as if he were being scored by a college debate panel. Kennedy, in full control, addressed the audience that really counted: the American people. Kennedy opened on a statesmanlike note similar to the one that Abraham Lincoln had sounded during the Civil War era. Referring to the enormous influence the Soviets exercised in international affairs, Kennedy maintained that the world could not endure half-slave and half-free.

Nixon opened by agreeing with Kennedy's statement, but he spent far too much time praising the progress made under the Eisenhower presidency and not enough outlining his own ideas of government.

Perhaps it did not really matter what Nixon said as he stood opposite John F. Kennedy that September in Chicago. It was what Americans saw that ultimately counted. Theodore H. White, covering the debates, recalled,

> the Vice-President as he half-slouched, his "Lazy Shave" powder faintly streaked with sweat, his eyes exaggerated hollows of blackness, his jaw, jowls, and face drooping with strain. . . . His normal shirt hung loosely about his neck, and his recent weight loss made him appear scrawny.

In the end the Kennedy-Nixon debate had little to do with issues, even though both candidates were well prepared for battle. The debates focused more on the personalities and images that were projected on the television screen. Kennedy wore a well-tailored dark suit; while Nixon wore a light suit in the first debate that seemed to melt his weakened image into the tiny TV screens of America.

Noting this emphasis, White complained, "Rarely in American history has there been a political campaign that discussed issues less or clarified them less. The TV debates . . . were the greatest opportunity ever for such a discussion, but it was an opportunity missed."

Most polls taken after the first debate gave the victory to Kennedy. However, most of those who listened to the debate

John F. Kennedy and Richard M. Nixon on the campaign trail, 1960
(John F. Kennedy Library)

on the radio believed that Nixon had won. The most extensive poll, conducted for CBS after the election by Dr. Elmo Roper, found that of four million Americans who said they had been decisively influenced by the TV debates, three million voted for Kennedy while only one million voted for Nixon. And as Kennedy himself said after the election, "It was TV more than anything else that turned the tide."

Although Nixon recovered somewhat in the later debates, no audience was as large as the first. The TV debates, perhaps more than anything else, set a precedent in American political history that lasts to this day. Arriving at the precise moment when the first TV generation was coming of voting age, they would ensure that televised debates would play an important role in our presidential politics for the rest of the century.

Kennedy was bolstered by the debates. He campaigned with renewed vigor and was greeted by growing and enthusiastic crowds across the country. His attitude toward his former poker partner was also changing. Kennedy told Professor John Kenneth Galbraith of Harvard, "When I first began this campaign, I just wanted to beat Nixon. Now I want to save the country from him."

Although Kennedy seemed to be winning the glamour and popularity contest, there could be no argument about where the national press was in the election. At a time when TV network news was still in its infancy, Nixon had the important support of an overwhelming majority of the nation's newspapers. The powerful Time-Life empire, controlled by media magnate Henry R. Luce, stood firmly behind Nixon's candidacy. Even though Nixon later came to distrust and even detest the press, he had to admit in 1960 that "the coverage of the campaign by newspapers has been very fair. I have no complaint on that score."

However, journalists covering the Nixon campaign noticed that the candidate at times seemed isolated and withdrawn. Peter Lisagor of the *Chicago Daily News* recalled, "He wouldn't see us. He began to isolate himself away from the press . . . he went into hiding in the Waldorf-Astoria Hotel for a couple of days and didn't even do any campaigning. There were some mystifying aspects to it. He brooded a great deal. He felt like he had been made the underdog and that the press was opposed to him."

That November, the popular vote was very close, with only 112,000 votes—less than 1 percent of the total—separating the candidates. But Nixon lost to Kennedy 303 to 219 in the electoral college. Kennedy was undoubtedly helped by a series of irregularities at the polls in two crucial states—Texas and Illinois. He also made important gains among black voters. The Kennedy brothers had boldly intervened during the campaign when civil rights leader Dr. Martin Luther King, Jr., was arrested for a traffic offense and sentenced to six months in a Georgia prison. Kennedy had called King's young wife, Coretta, to express concern for King's safety. Then his brother Robert called a Georgia judge to help arrange for Dr. King to be released on bond. Even King's father, a lifelong Republican and an influential black southern minister, voted for Kennedy. Black Americans never forgot what the Kennedys had done, and repaid them handsomely at the voting booths. When the election of 1960 was over, seven out of ten blacks had voted for Kennedy, and in urban sectors of the nation that tally was even higher. In Detroit, for example, Kennedy beat Nixon eight to one in the black community. Reflecting on his overall loss in 1960, Nixon later wrote, "I should have called the Judge, or done something similarly 'grandstand,' in the Martin Luther King case."

American Catholics too voted preponderantly for Kennedy, helping him carry important states in the Northeast. In addition, Kennedy may have defused whatever anti-Catholic sentiment there was in the country by appearing before the Greater Houston Ministerial Association in Texas during the campaign. Raising the religion issue himself, Kennedy told the meeting of Protestant ministers, "I believe in an America where the separation of church and state is absolute—where no Catholic prelate would tell the President (should he be a Catholic) how to act and no Protestant minister would tell his parishioners for whom to vote."

On the sticky question of religion, Nixon had said nothing. He had purposely avoided the religion issue, simply pretending it wasn't there. As Nixon later said with regret, "I should have personally repudiated Norman Vincent Peale [a prominent Protestant religious spokesman who had publicly stated that a Catholic president might possibly be under the influence of the Church in Rome], so as to win more Catholic votes. I should have made a speech at the end of the campaign attacking Kennedy for his systematic exploitation of the religious issue, so as to win more Protestant votes."

Thus, for the first time in American history, a Catholic candidate scored heavily with Protestant voters. Kennedy actually ended up with more Protestant votes than Nixon. And eight out of ten American Jews voted for Kennedy—a fact that Nixon never forgot. According to political scientist Stephen Isaacs, "The near solidarity of anti-Nixon sentiment among Jews in states like New York and Illinois may have resulted in the Kennedy victory." Clearly, American Jews did not hold Joseph P. Kennedy's overt anti-Semitism against his son. Few people, in 1960, knew that the vice president himself harbored some strangely bigoted views about Jews and their influence in American society and politics.

The only region of the country where Nixon did well was the South, where he was able to capitalize on a strong resentment of the big-city Democratic machine politicians. And, of course, there was the ingrained fear in the South that the election of John F. Kennedy would signal a sea change in race relations in that region. The civil rights movement was gaining momentum, and many southerners feared that it would grow even stronger with John F. Kennedy in the White House.

In the end the election of 1960 was a triumph of personality—John F. Kennedy's over Richard M. Nixon's. The Democratic Party's philosophy that government is to be used as a tool to help the nation's citizens collided head on with the Republican Party's philosophy that every citizen must bear some personal responsibility for his or her own well-being. But these heady philosophical issues were lost in the glitz and glitter of a media-driven campaign that, on the surface at least, revolved around the image and personalities of the two candidates.

John F. Kennedy and Jacqueline Kennedy greet Richard Nixon during the campaign of 1960. (John F. Kennedy Library)

Neither Kennedy nor Nixon was an ideologue or a true believer in his party's political dogma. More than anything else they were both symbolic postwar Americans on the way up—highly ambitious political men who tried to work the system. In 1960, one failed and one succeeded. One went to Washington to lead his nation and the free world while the other went into an early and uncomfortable retirement and into what appeared, by 1962, to be political oblivion. But history and politics are often unpredictable, and they were not yet quite through with Richard Nixon.

6

DEFEAT AND RENEWAL
Richard Nixon and the Election of 1968

"I leave you gentlemen now and you will all now write it. You will interpret it. That's your right. But as I leave you I want you to know—just think how much you're going to be missing. You won't have Nixon to kick around anymore, because, gentlemen, this is my last press conference."

"For the first time in seven years, I started not only to think seriously about running for the presidency again but to think where I should begin."

On December 14, 1960, President-elect John F. Kennedy flew to Key Biscayne, Florida, to meet with his defeated rival. Kennedy began the conversation with Nixon saying, "Well, it's hard to tell who won the election at this point." Because of the closeness of the race, Kennedy had come apparently to bring about some form of reconciliation. But the real motive behind Kennedy's visit, beyond offering Nixon an ambassadorship, was to find out if Nixon was going to contest the race. There were strong allegations of electioneering fraud in both Illinois (Mayor Richard Daley had allegedly manipulated some returns in some key Chicago area precincts) and Texas. There is good reason to believe that the allegations were accurate. Nixon lost Illinois and Texas by narrow margins, and wins in those two key states would have given him the presidency. Nixon, to his credit, did not want to ignite a constitutional crisis by demanding a recount that would have taken months in Illinois alone. Describing his decision not to contest the 1960 election, Nixon later said, "I wouldn't classify what I did as magnanimous or noble. Responsible would be my word for it. I simply did the right thing."

For the first time in 14 years Nixon did not know what to do with his life. Aside from closing down his office, saying goodbye to faithful staffers, and answering over 100,000 letters and wires, Nixon was initially at a loss. He became preoccupied with what he could have done and should have done to defeat Kennedy. This obsessive preoccupation with Kennedy (and the Kennedys) would haunt Nixon for the rest of his political and public life.

Within a few months of his defeat, Nixon left his family in Washington, D.C. (daughters Tricia and Julie were still in the middle of their school year) and returned to Southern California, where he joined a Los Angeles law firm. For Nixon, whose life had revolved around politics, going from vice president to private citizen was not easy. He took a small apartment, cooked his own meals, and spent much of his time brooding alone about what might have been. He watched, in anguish and great frustration, as the nation and the hated media began what was to become a three-year romance with Jack and Jacqueline Kennedy. As Nixon recalled in his memoirs,

> I had thought that I could move right into the work of the law firm, just as I had done with every other challenging new job. For several weeks, however, I found it difficult to concentrate and almost impossible to work up much enthusiasm. I realized I was experiencing the letdown of defeat.

That spring, in 1961, Pat and the children spent Easter vacation with Nixon near the ocean in Santa Monica. Slowly, the malaise of his 1960 defeat began to fade as Nixon took up his role as the titular head of the Republican Party. At the same time, he began to cast about for a political base in California. But the idea of running again for the House or the Senate was, in Nixon's own words, "an intolerable debasement" and "impossible."

For her part, Pat Nixon quickly readapted to the slower-paced and more relaxed California lifestyle. She busied herself with house decorating and settling Tricia and Julie into the fashionable private Marlborough School in Beverly Hills. Pat Nixon had little desire to return to a life in politics, which she had grown to detest while in Washington. As she told Samuel Goldwyn, Jr., at a Hollywood dinner party, "You think people in the movie business are competitive. They may be competitive but they are not mean. In politics, they are the most vicious people in the world."

While Nixon tried to decide how he could fit into California politics, he stayed abreast of affairs at the national and international levels. At his own request, he received frequent briefings from many government officials. For example, on April 19 and 20, 1961, in the midst of the Bay of Pigs crisis, Nixon met with Republican leaders on Capitol Hill and with Allen Dulles, director of the Central Intelligence Agency (CIA), who briefed him on foreign policy. An American-backed Cuban expeditionary force, funded, trained, and supplied by the CIA, had just failed in its abortive attempt to invade Cuba. This attempt to overthrow Fidel Castro, Cuba's Communist dictator, was a dismal embarrassment to the new and inexperienced government of John F. Kennedy.

But the real action on the political scene for Nixon was back in California, where the pressures were now mounting for him to run for governor in 1962. Even former president Eisenhower urged Nixon to run, saying, "If you don't run and the Republican candidate loses, you will be blamed for it, and you will be through as a national political leader."

At first, Nixon was torn about running for governor of California. He knew that if he ran and won, he would have a political base from which, if he chose, he could challenge Kennedy again in 1964. At the same time, Nixon had no interest in the mundane problems of California: water, education, pollution, and superhighways. His only real interest lay in the area of foreign policy, and he saw these state and local problems as boring. In addition, Nixon found that money was

Heavyweight champ Rocky Marciano (center) with Richard Nixon and John F. Kennedy (John F. Kennedy Library)

harder to come by when he returned to California. It was one thing to run for the presidency, with big donors eager to contribute money to a potential leader of the free world, and quite another to run for governor, even in a large state like California.

The early polls were encouraging, showing Nixon with a 20-point lead over the incumbent, Governor Pat Brown—57 percent to 37 percent. However, as Nixon later said, "The real problem was that I had no great desire to be governor of California. Equally compelling was my knowledge of how strongly Pat felt against my running." Pat Nixon had made it very clear that she did not want her husband to run. The girls were just entering adolescence and she wanted her husband home to help raise his daughters. She also hoped to spare the girls from the pain and cruelty of another campaign. Pat was made acutely aware of the difficulties inflicted on family life one day when Julie came home from school saying, "It hurts to be told your father stinks."

Finally, after an argument, Pat told her husband, "If you run this time, I'm not going to be out campaigning with you as I have in the past." At that point Nixon decided that he would not run. He was making some notes for a press conference to announce his decision when Pat relented. "I am more convinced than ever," she told him, "that if you run it will be a terrible mistake. But if you weigh everything and still decide to run, I will support your decision. I'll be there campaigning with you just as I always have."

Once again Nixon called on his former comrade-in-arms, Murray Chotiner, who encouraged his old chief to revert to the "Tricky Dick" style that had served Nixon so well in previous campaigns. Soon circulars and bumper stickers were popping up all over the state, asking the ugly question, "Is Brown pink?" This was a violation of state election law. Brown took the matter into the courts and obtained a restraining order against the Nixon camp. (The laws had been changed since the Douglas campaign.) The campaign then degenerated into a cacophony of name-calling and insinuation, and the press exposed Nixon's slipshod political tactics at every opportunity. Instead of designing his own programs for state improvement, Nixon called for a tax cut and a decrease in state spending, especially in mental hospitals, which Nixon callously described as "winter resorts" for "derelicts."

The Nixon candidacy hardly engendered a bandwagon in California. Prominent Republicans like Norris Poulson, the former mayor of Los Angeles, and Earl Warren, Jr., son of the chief justice of the U.S. Supreme Court, refused to support Nixon and instead endorsed his rival. The former Republican lieutenant governor, Harold J. Powers, called Nixon "a discard from the rubble heap of national politics." Polls soon showed Brown well ahead.

The Democrats also had their turncoats. A new face in Republican state politics, the popular Hollywood leading man Ronald Reagan, had once been a New Deal Democrat. Now registered as a Republican, Reagan traveled the state, giving speeches on behalf of Nixon. At the California Real Estate

Association convention, Reagan received an enthusiastic ovation from 2,500 realtors when he urged them to vote for Nixon.

The Democrats countered by bringing in some heavy artillery of their own: the president of the United States, John F. Kennedy; Vice President Johnson; and six members of the highly visible Kennedy cabinet all campaigned for Governor Brown. Nixon then brought in Eisenhower, who finally backed his former vice president uncategorically, saying, "I can personally vouch for his ability, his sense of duty, his sharpness of mind, his wealth in wisdom." As one of Nixon's aides remarked, "If he'd only given that speech two years ago, Dick Nixon would be President."

In the end, Nixon was the victim of a bad break as his efforts against Governor Brown came to be completely overshadowed by the dangerous Cuban Missile Crisis. On October 22 President Kennedy reported to the American people in a dramatic television address that the Soviets had moved medium-range nuclear missiles into Cuba. With the Cuban crisis dominating the news and the threat of nuclear war distracting voters in the last crucial weeks of the campaign, Nixon's chances of cutting into Brown's lead in the polls evaporated.

When the votes were tallied, Nixon lost by 297,000 votes out of almost 6 million. As Pat wept quietly in another room, Nixon watched in anguish as his last hope for a political career drifted away. He waited through the long night before deciding to offer a concession speech in what he was to bill as his "last press conference."

Nixon had been drinking heavily through the night and taking tranquilizers. He was obviously angry, upset, and agitated as he met with the press that morning. For the first time in public, a mean-spirited and ugly side of Richard Nixon became apparent. At times he was even incoherent. Convinced "the liberal press" was behind his losses to both Kennedy and Brown, Nixon decided to go out with a bombshell directed at the media. As he said in part,

> Never in my sixteen years of campaigning have I complained to a publisher, to an editor, about the coverage of a reporter. I believe a reporter has got a right to write it as he feels it. I believe if a reporter believes that one man ought to win rather than the other . . . he ought to say so.

> I will say to the reporters sometimes that I think, well, look, I wish you'd give my opponent the same going over that you gave me. And as I leave the press, all I can say is this: for sixteen years, ever since the Hiss case, you've had a lot of—a lot of fun—that you've had an opportunity to attack me, and I think I've given as good as I've taken. I leave you gentlemen now and you will all now write it. You will interpret it. That's your right. But as I leave you I want you to know—just think how much you're going to be missing. You won't have Nixon to kick around anymore, because, gentlemen, this is my last press conference.

The pundits now buried Richard Nixon. Syndicated reporter Mary McGrory, a longtime Nixon hater, wrote a column titled "Richard Nixon's Last Hurrah," in which she described his press appearance as "exit snarling." Five nights after the election, ABC newscaster Howard K. Smith hosted a half-hour TV special entitled "The Political Obituary of Richard Nixon."

California held little allure for Nixon after his loss. During a Florida vacation Nixon met his old friend Elmer Bobst, chairman of the board of the Warner-Lambert Pharmaceutical Company. Bobst advised Nixon to leave California and seek employment in New York, where opportunities in business for a well-connected lawyer who knew his way around Washington were far more lucrative than on the West Coast.

Nixon realized that moving to New York precluded any thought of an active role in politics in the near future. As he said, "A move to New York would mean giving up any thought of becoming a candidate for President in 1964, and running for any office in New York was out of the question." Nevertheless, a few months later the Nixons bought a 10-room coop in New York, and he joined a Wall Street law firm, which then became Nixon, Mudge, Rose, Guthrie, and Alexander.

Essentially, between 1962 and 1967 Richard Nixon became a private citizen living in political exile. When he traveled abroad, he was received cordially by many world leaders eager to pay their respects to a former vice president. In these years Nixon met with Francisco Franco of Spain, Charles De Gaulle of France, Gamal Abdel Nasser of Egypt, and Muhammad Ayub Khan of Pakistan, to name only a few. From the sidelines he continued to brood about the possibilities of what might have been. Though he had strong convictions about how to deal with some of the major problems facing the United States around the world, he was completely powerless to do anything about them.

Then, on November 22, 1963, fate in the form of an assassin's bullet altered American history for the rest of the century. That day Nixon had, ironically, just returned to New York from a business meeting in Dallas, Texas, when he learned during the taxi ride from the airport that President Kennedy had been assassinated in Dallas during the afternoon. The restless Nixon stayed up late into the next morning pondering the political fates and remembering the painful feeling of losing his own cherished brothers. He wrote a letter to the president's widow, Jacqueline Kennedy, thanking her for her services as first lady and adding, "In this tragic hour Pat and I want you to know that our thoughts and prayers are with you." A few weeks later, Mrs. Kennedy answered with a handwritten note thanking Nixon for his "most thoughtful letter" and advising him to cherish his family and the fact that he was alive.

Meanwhile, the Nixons were living well in New York on a basic salary of $220,000 a year. He was driven to work daily in a chauffeured black Cadillac, took long lunches at the best restaurants, and played golf at exclusive country clubs. In the presidential election of 1964, Nixon supported the Republican nominee, Arizona senator Barry Goldwater. Goldwater's conservative crusade for the presidency was doomed from the moment he crowed, "Extremism in the defense of liberty is no vice! . . . Moderation in the pursuit of justice is no virtue!" at the Republican convention. Although Richard Nixon presented Goldwater to the convention before his acceptance speech, he later reflected that "if he [Goldwater] had any chance to win the presidency, he lost it that night with that speech."

After Lyndon Johnson won the election in a landslide, Nixon and other party leaders called for a cooling-off period so that Republicans would be united for a possible congressional comeback in 1966. On January 9, 1965, after a small family party celebrating his 52nd birthday, Nixon began to think about his own political future. He reflected that Winston Churchill had been in his mid-fifties when he lost his position of leadership in the British House of Commons in 1929. Churchill, Nixon remembered, had also been written off politically. But he had refused to accept the verdict of the so-called experts and had risen to become one of the towering political leaders of the 20th century. Sitting in his comfortable study, Nixon stared deeply into the crackling fire as he wrote down a list of his New Year's resolutions for 1965. "For the first time in seven years," Nixon would later recall, "I started not only to think seriously about running for the presidency again but to think where I should begin."

By the spring of 1968 Richard Nixon found his opening as the country teetered on the brink of what can best be described as a national nervous breakdown.

With American cities imploding all around him—between 1965 and 1967 there had been major riots in Los Angeles, Detroit, and Newark—President Lyndon Johnson had only one vague hope for somehow salvaging his doomed presidency: a solution to the war in Southeast Asia. But Johnson, to his everlasting discredit, became more and more isolated as he circled the wagons around the White House over Vietnam. Instead of listening to the well-intentioned and reasoned arguments of his growing legion of critics, Johnson became a lonely and solitary figure who, forced to rely on the distortions of field commanders and Pentagon bureaucrats, never understood the terrible toll the war in Vietnam was taking on the collective psyche of the American people.

The straw that broke Johnson's political back was the Tet offensive of January 1968—a massive Vietcong and North Vietnamese counterattack directed against American forces during Tet, the Vietnamese lunar New Year. In Saigon, South Vietnam's capital, the American embassy grounds were actually occupied for several hours. The Tet offensive was, in fact, a military failure for the Communists, who suffered 42,300 soldiers killed—one-third of their entire strike force. But for President Johnson, Tet was a public relations nightmare of disastrous proportions: the American people watched news footage in horror, seeing retreating American troops apparently overrun by the Communists. Tet was to be the death knell of Lyndon Johnson's presidency. On March 31 the dejected president appeared on national television to announce that he had called for a halt to the bombing of most of North Vietnam, and he asked North Vietnam to begin negotiating a settlement that would end the war. Then, still reeling from the embarrassment of the New Hampshire primary on March 12, where Senator Eugene McCarthy polled 42.4 percent of the vote to the president's 49.5 percent, Johnson shocked the nation and the world by announcing that he would not be a candidate for reelection in 1968.

Less than a week later, the Reverend Martin Luther King, Jr., was assassinated while visiting Memphis, Tennessee, to help settle a strike by sanitation workers. King, who had been the embodiment of the conscience of the struggle for civil rights

Martin Luther King, Jr. His assassination in 1968 brought on violence that benefited Richard Nixon's stand on law and order. (Boston University)

in the United States, was seen by many black Americans as the victim of a massive conspiracy. In the days following the assassination, blacks rioted in 168 cities and towns across the nation, burning and looting white-owned businesses and property. More than 50,000 federal and National Guard troops were called out to quell the violence. Almost 20,000 people were arrested, and 39 people were killed.

Following on the heels of the riots, student protests erupted all over the United States. Between January and June 1968 more than 200 demonstrations disrupted normal academic life at virtually every major institution of higher learning. In New York City, protesting students who represented one of the major antiwar groups, the Students for a Democratic Society (SDS), occupied the office of the president of Columbia University and other college buildings for 10 days. Private files were trashed and, in at least one case, the students destroyed a professor's lifetime of research.

Most Americans were, of course, immune from the violence and upheavals that spring. But they could watch in dismay from the comfort of their living rooms as the sequence of shocking events continued to unfold on nightly television newscasts. As the *Columbia Journalism Review* reported, the nightly news "made social disorganization a realistic threat to the comfortably-off middle-class urbanites, to suburbanites, to rural residents—to all those . . . who have seldom faced robbery, mugging, protest marching . . . black power salutes, or perhaps even hostile questions about their values."

Into the breach stepped Richard Nixon. To a nation on the brink of social, political, and cultural breakdown, as Theodore H. White pointed out, "Richard Nixon rested his thrust on stability rather than on dynamism." As White wrote,

> The situation was clear as early as January of the year: The country was torn, the consensus of Lyndon Johnson had dissolved, the administration had lost the confidence of the American people, the apparently hopeless war went on. The situation insisted on alternative national leadership. . . . No one could claim greater credit from the [Republican] Party's non-commissioned officers than Richard M. Nixon. Had it been a vote within an army, the Party regulars would have chosen Richard Nixon as their corps commander.

Only one man stood between Nixon and a Republican victory in 1968: Robert F. Kennedy. The brother of the martyred president, Kennedy had finally left the Johnson administration in disgust and despair. The former attorney general had been elected a U.S. senator from New York and had broken bitterly with Johnson over Vietnam in 1966 when the *New York Times* reported a Kennedy speech with the headline, "KENNEDY BIDS US OFFER VIETCONG A ROLE IN SAIGON." By 1967, according to Theodore H. White, Kennedy was calling the war "a waste, an extravagance, an excess, a diversion of all the country's resources . . . which was crippling it to deal with problems at home." But Kennedy was initially reluctant to tear the Democratic Party apart by mounting a campaign against a sitting president who was still the titular leader of his party.

However, in the aftermath of the Tet offensive, Kennedy began to waver under pressure from former John F. Kennedy loyalists and leaders of the antiwar movement. On March 15, 1968, after watching McCarthy embarrass the president in the New Hampshire primary, Kennedy announced his decision to run for the presidency.

The Kennedy announcement split the antiwar activists down the middle. Kennedy's opponents in the movement viewed his candidacy as a blatant act of treachery toward senator Eugene McCarthy, who had carried the antiwar banner long before Kennedy had entered the political fray. McCarthy himself seemed publicly unmoved by Kennedy's announcement, but he was privately outraged.

All of this worked to the advantage of the Republicans, who looked stronger day by day as antiwar protesters kept Johnson a prisoner in his own White House while they chanted outside, "Hey, hey, LBJ, How many kids did you kill today?" The stability promised by the Republicans began to look appealing to much of middle America. By the spring, Nixon's major opponents in the Republican Party, Governor Nelson Rockefeller of New York and Governor George Romney of Michigan (who claimed to have been "brainwashed" on a visit to Vietnam), had dropped out, leaving a fairly clear field as Nixon picked up one primary win after another. Still overly preoccupied with the Kennedy mystique, Nixon agonized over the possibility of having to face yet another Kennedy in a presidential contest.

Bobby Kennedy appeared to have unlimited stamina and energy. It seemed he was everywhere. In a single week Kennedy appeared in Kansas, Alabama, Washington, Tennessee, New York, California, Oregon, Idaho, Utah, Nebraska, and Colorado. The media were having a field day as Kennedy traversed the country, drawing huge, adoring crowds of young people and students.

By April and May, polling data revealed that Kennedy was ahead of McCarthy, and it looked as if the California primary in June would take Kennedy over the top in the Democratic Party.

The Kennedy campaign began to take on the air of a crusade as thousands of students who had been "Clean for Gene (McCarthy)" in the New Hampshire snows flocked to climb on the Kennedy bandwagon. Instead of attacking Nixon and the Republicans, however, Kennedy leveled his verbal assaults on the Johnson administration, hoping to undercut support for Johnson's vice president, Hubert Humphrey, who was now seen as the Democratic Party's establishment candidate for the presidency. "Our country is in danger . . . not just from the foreign enemies but above all from our own misguided policies," Kennedy said. He labeled President Johnson a sinister man "calling upon the darker impulses of the American spirit." His inflammatory rhetoric began to frighten party regulars. As Theodore H. White recalled, Kennedy began to be

> Carried away by his own emotions and their echo among the volatile cheering young, he could not quite grasp how television outlined his figure on the forty-second and one-minute snatches of evening news shows where the larger, national, mature audience saw him: hysterical, high-pitched, hair blowing in the wind, almost demoniac, frightening . . .

Once again, however, fate intervened on Nixon's behalf. On June 5, the night of the California primary, Robert F. Kennedy was shot by a young Palestinian who was outraged over Kennedy's support for Israel. Kennedy died the next day. Nixon attended the funeral mass at St. Patrick's Cathedral in New York. By the end of June, Nixon was back on the campaign trail.

In July, at the Republican National Convention in Miami, Nixon easily overcame token opposition from Nelson Rockefeller, Governor Ronald Reagan of California, and Mayor John Lindsay of New York. Nixon was nominated with 692 votes, 25 more than he needed. After narrowing his vice presidential choices down to the obscure governors Spiro T. Agnew of Maryland and John Volpe of Massachusetts, Nixon chose Agnew. The road back had been long and arduous, but Nixon had made it once again. With Pat beaming by his side, he proudly accepted his party's nomination with an emotional appeal to all Americans:

> Tonight I see the face of a child. He lives in a great city. He's black or he's white, he's Mexican, Italian, Polish. None of that matters. What matters is he's an American child, and he dreams the dreams of a child. And yet when he awakens, he awakens to a living nightmare of poverty, neglect and despair. He fails in school, he ends up on welfare. For him the American system is one that feeds his stomach and starves his soul. It breaks his heart. And in the end it may take his life on some distant battlefield.

That August the Democrats' doom was sealed by the Democrats themselves. The front-runner was Vice President Hubert H. Humphrey. But instead of a coronation, the Democratic National Convention in Chicago turned into an all-out assault by Chicago police against the Yippies (Youth International Party) and the thousands of antiwar protesters who had made their way to Chicago to express their outrage at what they called "Lyndon and Hubert's celebration of death." Mayor Daley had assigned 12,000 Chicago police, decked out in full riot gear, to patrol the streets around the convention site. Another 12,000 army troops and Illinois National Guard units were on call, armed with rifles, bazookas, and flamethrowers. To those watching in the United States and around the world, it appeared that America had declared war on its children.

In Grant Park and along Michigan Avenue, the police began to attack and savagely beat anyone they could get their hands on. After some objects were thrown at them from the Hilton Hotel, the police actually charged into the building, beating and clubbing people in the corridors and breaking into rooms.

Hubert Humphrey didn't get it. Although the vice president was a good and decent man, he was too busy politicking to ever take time to smell the stinging and acrid aroma of the tear gas that wafted into the hotels and even onto the convention floor itself. On the floor of the convention, only Senator Abraham Ribicoff of Connecticut had the good sense to decry the "Gestapo tactics in the streets of Chicago" and denounce Mayor Daley. From the Illinois delegation, Daley shouted an obscenity and led a chorus of booing.

Humphrey chose Senator Edmund Muskie of Maine as his running mate. But Humphrey and the Democratic Party did not have time to regroup or recover from the shocking violence of the Chicago convention. Humphrey's decision to turn to "politics as usual" doomed the happy warrior from Minnesota before his campaign against Richard Nixon had even gotten off the ground. Most American voters, according to the polls, demonstrated little enthusiasm for either Nixon or Humphrey. Even with the conservative Alabama governor, George C. Wallace, in the race, running on the American Independent Party ticket, Nixon knew that if he could run a mistake-free campaign, this time he would have an excellent chance of winning.

Nixon surrounded himself with advertising men who carefully packaged their candidate as if he were a box of breakfast cereal. Nixon rarely visited college campuses or urban ghettos, where he might get a hostile reception. With Murray Chotiner and other slick television producers carefully orchestrating all of his public appearances, Nixon was like a butterfly in a cocoon—basically unreachable by the average American voter. When Nixon did appear in what looked to be a public format, even the audiences and panelists had been carefully selected for sex, race, and religion. As Joe McGinnis noted in *The Selling of the President 1968*, one cynical observer said, "Nixon had not only developed the use of the platitude, he's raised it to an art form. It's mashed potatoes. It appeals to the lowest common denominator of American taste. It's a farce, a delicious farce; self-deception carried to the nth degree." The Nixon ad men would trot out celebrities like Jackie Gleason, Billy Graham, and American icon John Wayne to endorse Nixon. As Nixon strategist Kevin Phillips pointed out, "Wayne might sound bad to people in New York, but he sounds great to the schmucks we're trying to reach through John Wayne. The people down there along the Yahoo Belt."

For all his slick packaging, Nixon saw his lead begin to evaporate in the final weeks as the Humphrey campaign gained ground on domestic policy issues. The election of 1968 turned out to be extremely close, with Nixon beating Humphrey 31,770,237 to 31,270,533—a tiny margin of 499,704 votes (George Wallace polled almost 10 million votes). But the popular numbers actually belied the results. The American people had rejected the Democratic Party and the policies of Lyndon Johnson. Richard Nixon had swept 32 states, beating Humphrey 301 to 191 in the electoral college. Just four years after the Goldwater debacle of 1964, the political fortunes of Richard Nixon and the Republican Party had been revived by the tumultuous tragedies of 1968.

At his New York apartment on Fifth Avenue, Nixon could finally relax for the first time in many months. He put on one of his favorite pieces of music: the score from the classic TV documentary of World War II, *Victory at Sea*. As he recalled,

> The battle had been long and arduous. We had suffered reverses and won victories. The struggle had been hard fought. But now we had won the final victory. The music captured the moment for me better than anything I could say or think or write.

Richard Nixon had accomplished his ultimate political dream: the presidency of the United States. But he did not have a national mandate. He was, because of George Wallace's strong showing, a minority president of a badly divided nation. He was taking over a country that was reeling from war, assassination, crime, poverty, racism, and alienated youth. It was a country that needed the tender touch of a leader who could heal. In 1969 Richard Nixon would finally have the power. But it remained to be seen whether he would use it wisely or well.

7

IN POWER
Richard Nixon and Vietnam

> "I will not be the first president of the United States to lose a war."

With the 1968 election behind him, Richard Nixon set to work shaping his new government and completed his cabinet appointments by December 11. Nixon did not see his cabinet as the center of power in his new administration. He had attended hundreds of cabinet meetings as vice president and watched as little was accomplished. His appointments met with general approval, though as Stephen E. Ambrose pointed out, "there were no blacks, no women, no Jews, no Democrats and no Rockefellers. . . . the Cabinet was praised as moderate and middle-of-the-road. The members were self-made men, highly successful either in business or politics."

Only two appointments proved to have a lasting impact on national affairs. For the key post of attorney general, Nixon chose his New York law partner and friend John Mitchell. "Mitchell," Nixon said, "was tough, intelligent, and fair. I wanted someone who shared my concern about permissiveness in the courts and even in many law enforcement agencies.... Moreover, I counted him my most trusted friend and adviser and I wanted to have his advice available, not just on legal matters but on the whole range of presidential decision-making."

In the Nixon administration, the key advisory post in foreign policy was not to be in the State Department, which was headed by William Rogers. As Nixon said, "From the outset of my administration . . . I planned to direct foreign policy from the White House." Thus, the position of National Security Adviser to the president became a key post that Nixon decided to structure in his own way and that he viewed as "crucial." For that position Nixon chose Dr. Henry Kissinger, a professor of government at Harvard University whose influential book *Nuclear Weapons and Foreign Policy* had become somewhat of a cold war primer on maintaining the dangerous and delicate balance of power in the atomic age. Kissinger had served for many years as a foreign policy adviser to Nelson Rockefeller, and there had been little love lost between the Rockefeller wing of the party and the Nixonians. Kissinger had even made disparaging remarks about Nixon in private. He viewed Nixon as "an anti-Communist fanatic," and called him "the most dangerous of all the men running, to have as president." But as president, Nixon was able to put all this aside and hire Dr. Kissinger, a Jewish refugee from the Nazis who still spoke with a heavy German accent, to head the National Security Council. As Nixon stated, "I had a strong intuition about Henry Kissinger. . . . The combination was unlikely—the grocer's son from Whittier and the refugee from Hitler's Germany, the politician and the academic. But our differences helped make the partnership work."

When Nixon took the oath of office on January 20, 1969, the United States was hardly a nation at peace. In fact, the country was hardly united. Violence and division had made the 1960s one of the most tumultuous decades of the 20th century for America. The country had been rocked by assassination, racial upheaval, and urban and political violence. From Cambridge, Massachusetts, to Berkeley, California, American college campuses had seen student riots and unrest. Richard Nixon had inherited a country torn apart by racial division, social dislocation, and, most of all, by the nation's seemingly endless

First Lady Pat Nixon and President Richard M. Nixon (Richard Nixon Library)

involvement in a foreign war that very few Americans either understood or wanted: the war in Vietnam.

Between 1961 and 1969, more than 31,000 Americans had been killed in Vietnam. The war had cost the lives of hundreds of thousands of Vietnamese, not to mention the maimed and wounded (civilian as well as military). Billions of dollars (24 billion in fiscal 1969 alone) from the national treasury had been poured down the seemingly bottomless pit of this ugly war that appeared to many Americans both wrong and unwinnable. Vociferous dissent over the war had already driven one president from office. Now the war was Nixon's problem.

As a first-term senator, Nixon (accompanied by his wife) had visited Southeast Asia in 1953, when the region was still under

French control. He had traveled through jungle terrain, stopping off at refugee camps and dining with French officers. Nixon could hear the sound of mortar fire while meeting for briefings with friendly Vietnamese troops. But, like many American officials who travel quickly through a foreign nation and see only what they are allowed or supposed to see, Nixon misread the conflict and saw it in the simplistic terms of the struggle between communism and democracy. Ever the cold warrior, Nixon told his Vietnamese hosts "that they were fighting on the very outpost of freedom and that the American people supported their cause and honored their heroism." Deeply impressed with the role of the Vietnamese in the struggle against communism, Nixon left Southeast Asia convinced that the war could be won if only the French could be made to feel the same resolve that inspired him. As he later recalled,

> I left Vietnam, Laos, and Cambodia convinced that the French had failed primarily because they had not sufficiently trained, much less inspired, the Indochinese people to be able to defend themselves. They had failed to build a cause—or a cadre—that could resist the nationalist and anticolonialist appeals of the Communists.

In the 19th century the French had colonized Vietnam, Laos, and Cambodia, known in those days as French Indochina. After World War II, the French colonialists were opposed by Ho Chi Minh, a Vietnamese nationalist who was also a Communist. Ho had seized Hanoi, the capital city in the North, in 1945, and had declared the independent state of the Democratic Republic of Vietnam. The French soon began an attempt to restore authority and control over the North by military action.

At first, the United States took little interest in the struggle between the French and the insurgent Vietnamese. But as the French situation worsened, the United States found itself more deeply embroiled in the cold war with the Soviet Union and Communist China (the Communists had seized mainland China in 1949). Thus, in the late 1940s and early 1950s, the Truman administration found itself supporting the French and contributing about 40 percent of the war's cost, following a State Department recommendation that "all practicable measures be taken to prevent further Communist expansion in Southeast Asia."

By the time the French were finally defeated at the Battle of Dienbienphu in 1954, the United States was footing 80 percent of the cost of the war. At the peace conference, the Eisenhower administration managed to get Indochina divided into four parts: Laos and Cambodia became independent; Vietnam was partitioned into North and South Vietnam, with the northern half controlled from Hanoi by the Communists under Ho Chi Minh and the southern portion ruled from Saigon as the Republic of Vietnam. It was also agreed that a free national election would be held in 1956.

The anticommunist leader of South Vietnam, Premier Ngo Dinh Diem, was not politically strong enough to win a national election against his enemy Ho Chi Minh. Ho was seen by many of the people, especially the peasants, as the father of Vietnamese independence. So Diem refused to hold the elections that had been promised to unify the divided country. With American aid, Diem was strong enough to rule from Saigon and to fight the Communists, who by 1960 had organized the National Liberation Front (NLF), called the Viet Cong by the Americans.

After 1961, under President Kennedy, American involvement in Vietnam began to escalate out of control. Influenced by Secretary of Defense Robert McNamara, Secretary of State Dean Rusk, and General Maxwell D. Taylor, who argued that the Communists could be checked by sufficient military power, President Kennedy finally agreed to send "military advisers" to Vietnam. These tough-minded members of the Kennedy administration were convinced that the presence of overwhelming American military might and superiority would easily quell any form of organized resistance in a country as backward as Vietnam. But these technocrats were wrong. The Communists in Vietnam, who viewed their struggle as a civil war as well as an effort to rid their land of foreign control and imperialistic domination, fought back, and American military personnel were drawn slowly but inexorably into the vortex of what became the greatest tragedy in modern American history. By 1962 there were 12,000 American troops in South Vietnam. Still the Viet Cong, despite their brutality in the countryside, continued to gain ground against the Saigon regime. And by the time of Kennedy's assassination in November 1963, there were 16,000 Americans in Vietnam.

Under President Johnson, American combat strength had increased from 16,000 to 550,000 troops over a five-year period. Nixon thought he understood where Johnson and the remaining Kennedy men in his administration had gone wrong. As Nixon said, "Against his [Johnson's] better instincts . . . he refused to give his military commanders the authority to conduct the war in a way that would have won it. He desperately wanted to end the war by negotiations."

But Nixon, too, misunderstood the resolve that existed among the North Vietnamese and the peasant guerrilla fighters in the South. Declaring "I will not be the first president of the United States to lose a war," Nixon had pledged during the election campaign that he had a secret plan to end the conflict. However, Nixon had never been forced to specify the exact nature of his plan.

As president, Nixon would seek the support of his "silent majority"—those in Middle America who he felt had helped elect him and who still supported American involvement in the war. Nixon would unleash his vice president, Spiro T. Agnew, to attack the media and other critics of the war. In effect, Agnew became, as David Halberstam observed, "Nixon's Nixon." Agnew's role was also to rid Congress of dovish critics—that is, as David Halberstam wrote in *The Best and the Brightest,* "to remove from the Congress those men most opposed to a war Nixon was supposed to be ending." As *Washington Post* reporter Don Oberdorfer wrote, "What President Nixon means by peace is what other people mean by victory."

On his first restless night as president of the United States, Richard Nixon got only four hours' sleep. Awake by 6:45 A.M., Nixon was shaving when he recalled that shortly after the election President Johnson had shown him a hidden safe. Opening the safe, Nixon found the daily Vietnam Situation Report that had been compiled for the president by the various intelligence services. As he read through the report he came to the latest casualty figures. During the week ending January 18, 1969, 185 Americans had been killed and 1,237 wounded in Vietnam. From January 1, 1968, to January 18, 1969, 14,958 had been killed and 95,798 had been wounded. These cold statistics must have struck Nixon numb. He now knew that every American killed from that day on would be the responsibility of his presidency. Clearly, if he had a plan to end the war, it should be put into immediate motion.

But as Henry Kissinger's power and influence within the Nixon White House increased, the administration adopted a new foreign policy initiative that would hinder American withdrawal from Southeast Asia. The new policy, the "Nixon doctrine," was designed to calm the fears of domestic critics and foreign allies alike who worried that in the rush to get out of Vietnam, the United States might, in Kissinger's words, "shed all its responsibilities and turn its back on all interests in the region."

President Richard M. Nixon, 37th president of the United States (Richard Nixon Library)

As Kissinger conceived of it, the Nixon doctrine was a firm warning, to friends and foes alike, that the United States intended to hold fast to its anticommunist commitments around the world. At the same time, the United States would somehow avoid becoming dangerously bogged down in a land war that required a massive commitment of troops, as President Johnson had done in Vietnam. As Kissinger said, "At the highest level of the threat, we had to make explicit our unchanged opposition to the aggressive designs of any major power in Asia. At the low end of the spectrum we had to avoid being involved in civil wars."

While Kissinger was busy manipulating policy behind the scenes, Nixon was still saddled with the immediate burden of the war in Vietnam and the restless and violent forces that the war had unleashed among the American people. Realizing that he was not bound by the war as his predecessor had been, Nixon envisioned a gradual disengagement that would be compatible with his foreign policy and the aims of his presidency: he called it "Vietnamization."

As peace talks between American diplomats and the North Vietnamese got underway in Paris, Nixon proposed to withdraw American troops no matter how the Paris talks progressed. But this was essentially a Nixon ploy, an example of how American leaders since President Kennedy have manipulated the English language in order to confuse the public. "Vietnamization" simply meant replacing American troops with Vietnamese troops. Thus, instead of American boys killing Asian boys, the Nixon solution was for Asian boys to kill Asian boys using American resources. The bottom line was that the killing was to continue. As historian William L. O'Neill wryly observed in his book *Coming Apart*, "President Nixon meant to wage war on the cheap."

By late 1969 and early 1970, although American troop strength was still well over 400,000 in Vietnam, American casualties and costs may well have been declining. But people were still dying. As O'Neill said, "In the short run Vietnamization was a great success. The war was less expensive in lives and dollars." Also, by reducing American middle-class anxiety over the draft by instituting a lottery system in which potential draftees who pulled high numbers had only a slim chance of being called up for military service (which only served to confuse the war's leading protesters), Nixon had successfully, for a while anyway, muted his most vocal opponents.

But in the spring of 1970, the Nixon administration seriously miscalculated the resolve of the antiwar movement, which, while in disarray, was still very much alive on almost every college campus. It was this fundamental failure to comprehend the depth of antiwar sentiment among so many young people that would ultimately lead the Nixon White House down a path of dangerous criminal excess from which there would be no return and through which the president himself would eventually be brought down.

The process of decline began on April 30, 1970, when President Nixon appeared on national television to announce that the United States had launched what the president called an "incursion" into Cambodia, a neighbor of South Vietnam on the western border.

During the early weeks of April the armies of Ho Chi Minh had pushed into Cambodia as they infiltrated down the Ho Chi Minh Trail into South Vietnam. While it wasn't clear whether Ho's troops were merely seeking to escape American and South Vietnamese forces or actually trying to cause trouble in Cambodia, Nixon and his advisers worried that the Communists would capture Phnom Penh, Cambodia's capital. Like President Johnson before him, Nixon believed in the domino theory—one country after another falling to the Communists—and he did not want to preside over the loss of Cambodia. Thus, on April 16, Nixon ordered the CIA to give all-out support to the Cambodian government, to send in more money and to turn over captured arms to the Cambodian army so that they might defend themselves against Communist aggression. He sent an urgent message to Kissinger saying "we need a bold move in Cambodia to show that we stand with Lon Nol." (General Lon Nol had overthrown Cambodian ruler Prince Sihanouk in a bloodless coup on March 18, 1970.) As Nixon said, "They [the Communists] are romping in there, and the only government in Cambodia in the last twenty-five years that had the guts to take a pro-Western and pro-American stand is ready to fall."

Student protests against Nixon's decision to go into Cambodia were immediate and fierce. The president was soon so unwelcome on college campuses that he had to cancel plans to attend his daughter Julie's graduation from Smith College and his son-in-law David Eisenhower's graduation from Amherst College.

As word spread from campus to campus, antiwar student groups mobilized in a concerted effort against the Nixon administration's new and aggressive policies in Cambodia. One university after another began to go on strike and shut down. Final exams and closing days of classes were canceled and replaced with teach-ins and calls for student action (violent and nonviolent). In some cases, professors who refused to cancel their classes were either threatened or intimidated by students, some of whom had little interest in the war and only saw the episodic flow of events as a golden opportunity to avoid finals and enjoy an early vacation.

Most student protesters were, however, legitimately outraged by Nixon's foreign policy, especially after the president ordered renewed air strikes against North Vietnam. Instead of addressing the concerns of the sincere young antiwar people, Nixon condemned all the students as troublemakers and threw oil on the fires of their raging protests.

On the morning of May 1, Nixon visited the Pentagon for a firsthand briefing from the Joint Chiefs of Staff. In a blatant show of insensitivity and disrespect, the president of the United States publicly blurted out his deep-seated resentment of the students:

> You see these bums, you know, blowing up the campuses. Listen, the boys that are on the college campuses today are the luckiest people in the world, going to the greatest universities, and here they are burning up the books, I mean storming around about this issue—I mean you name it—get rid of the war; there will be another one.

Three days later, on May 4, 1970, Ohio National Guard units on the campus of Kent State University fired blindly into a crowd of antiwar protesters, killing four students. Although the young guardsmen were not threatened by the unarmed students, the tense nationwide atmosphere had given some misguided officer the idea that young people and students were the enemy, and so the order was given to open fire. Some of the dead and wounded had not even been involved in the antiwar rally and had merely been changing classes. Once again, Nixon misunderstood the depths of student despair and the nature of campus protest. He compounded the Kent State tragedy when he had his press secretary, Ron Ziegler, read a statement to the White House press corps:

> This should remind us all once again that when dissent turns to violence, it invites tragedy. It is my hope this tragic and unfortunate incident will strengthen the determination of all the Nation's campuses—administrators, faculty, and students alike—to stand firmly for the right which exists in this country of peaceful dissent and just as strongly against the resort to violence as a means of such expression.

For one thing, the students at Kent State had been engaged in a peaceful protest. If anyone had contributed to the climate of violence that was sweeping the country, it was the president who had called the protesting students "bums." The father of 19-year-old Allison Krause, an innocent student who had been killed, drew the sympathy of many Americans when he put his family's tragedy into terse and understandable perspective in contrast to Nixon's incendiary remarks: "My child," Krause said, "was not a bum."

Of course, the violence in 1970 was not waged only by the official forces of repression. Radical groups like the Black Panthers and Weathermen (students who had broken with the SDS to pursue a policy of violent revolution) were engaged in an unofficial campaign of haphazard violence and terror. In 1970 the New York offices of Mobil, IBM, General Telephone, and various banks had been bombed or robbed. In March a homemade bomb factory had blown up in Greenwich Village, killing three young radicals.

The weekend following the Kent State tragedy, more than 250 striking colleges planned to send students and faculty to Washington to publicly protest the events of that spring. Like his predecessor Lyndon Johnson, Richard Nixon had become an isolated president, with the wagons (in this case hundreds of buses to ward off the threat of violence) circled around the embattled White House.

As the campuses closed and emptied out across the country, some protests became increasingly violent. In many cities students rampaged through nearby neighborhoods vandalizing stores, breaking windows, and, in a few cases, setting buildings on fire. Clearly, the Cambodian invasion and Kent State had set off a new wave of turmoil in the nation.

Meanwhile, Nixon began to comprehend that, after years of student discontent with the war, he had unleashed a powerful genie that might ultimately be difficult to get back into the bottle. The president became more aware that the average American was increasingly shocked and frightened as the upheavals around the country were being reported night after night on the TV news. Nixon may have been insensitive, but he wasn't stupid. On May 5 he met with congressional committees to explain his position on Cambodia. He believed that by taking his message to Congress, he would ultimately be reaching the American people. He pledged to withdraw American troops from Cambodia in three to seven weeks. He also promised that no American soldier would be sent deeper than 21 miles into Cambodia.

As the weekend of protest approached, the violence escalated. In New York a group of hard-hat construction workers, angered by the campus riots, attacked antiwar protesters in the financial district. These men, outraged that Mayor John Lindsay had lowered the American flag to half-staff after Kent State, stormed the building where demonstrations were taking place and beat up students and anyone with long hair while New York police stood by and did nothing.

On Friday, May 9, as thousands of students from all over the nation descended on Washington, D.C., Nixon called a press conference over the objections of his staff, hoping to defuse what was potentially a disastrous confrontation—an onslaught against the president in the nation's capital. When asked what he thought the students wanted, Nixon replied in a conciliatory tone: "They are trying," the president said, "to say that they want peace. They are trying to say that they want to stop the killing. . . . They are trying to say that we ought to get out of Vietnam. I agree with everything that they are trying to accomplish."

By early Saturday morning Washington took on the look of a city under a state of siege. The mood of the city was surreal as armed soldiers nervously patrolled the streets and surrounded the White House in front of the barricade of empty buses. Federal agents and marshals in plainclothes were everywhere and didn't even attempt to make themselves unobtrusive. Inside the White House, the president, his family, and his aides looked nervously out the windows. They could see the gathering crowds of students in Lafayette Park across Pennsylvania Avenue. They could see the soldiers massing and the TV units being set up everywhere as thousands of young people streamed into the capital, preparing to camp out for the night in anticipation of the next day's demonstrations against the war and the policies of the Nixon administration.

As Nixon recalled in his memoirs, "I felt that we should do everything possible to make sure that this event was nonviolent and that we did not appear insensitive to it." Even the president's usually combative domestic policy adviser, John Ehrlichman, urged the president to communicate in some fashion with the demonstrators. On the other hand, Henry Kissinger, ever disdainful of policy conducted because of anger on campus, urged Nixon to take a hard line so that American foreign policy would not be shaped by protesters taking to the streets.

That night Nixon slept very fitfully, and he awakened well before dawn. For a time he went to the Lincoln Sitting Room, where he tried to relax by listening to classical music. Peering out the window into the early morning gloom and darkness, he could still see small groups of young people gathering at the Ellipse between the White House and the Washington Monument. Nixon's longtime valet, Manuel (Manolo) Sanchez, came in to see if the president wanted some tea or coffee. On a whim, Nixon asked Sanchez if he had ever been to the Lincoln Memorial at night. Sanchez said he had never seen the monument lit up in the darkness, and Nixon replied, "Let's go look at it now."

At 4:35 A.M. Nixon and his valet left the White House with a petrified Secret Service detail. Nixon insisted that none of his aides be informed (although, to his frustration, this order was not obeyed and two harried aides, Ron Ziegler and Egil "Bud" Krogh, soon caught up with their boss). At about 4:40 A.M. the president, like any other tourist, casually but briskly walked up the steps of the Lincoln Memorial.

To the utter astonishment of a small group of eight students from upstate New York who had camped out under the memorial, there was the president of the United States walking toward them with his hand outstretched. According to Nixon, the students "were not unfriendly. As a matter of fact, they seemed somewhat overawed, and, of course, quite surprised."

In order to put the youngsters at ease, Nixon made small talk by asking how many of them had visited the nation's capital before. "To get the conversation going," Nixon wrote in a confidential May 13 memo to Bob Haldeman, "I asked them how old they were, what they were studying, the usual questions."

Nixon told the students that his objective was not to invade Cambodia but to get out of Vietnam. He said that he hoped that they would not allow their hatred of the war to turn them against their country and the whole system of government. The students, for the most part, said little. "I know that probably most of you think I'm an SOB," the president then said, "but I want you to know that I understand just how you feel."

Nixon urged the students to travel to see the world while they were still young. As dawn broke over the besieged capital, Nixon greeted some newly arriving students and shook some more hands. When one young woman told him that she was from Syracuse University, the president praised the Syracuse football team. Before he left, Nixon made certain to remind the students, "Remember this is a great country, with all of its faults." Then he got into his car and drove to the Capitol, where he gave Sanchez a tour of the empty chambers in the building where he had once labored as a young congressman.

Clearly, this was a president under tremendous stress and pressure. But Nixon, basically a shy man, had not comported himself poorly in his meeting with the students. Unlike Lyndon Johnson, Nixon had done his best to communicate across the generation gap even if his policies were indefensible and even heinous to his young critics. The press, however, distorting the overall reality of Nixon's encounter with the students, reported that the president had talked to them about sports when they had traveled all night to protest against the war and his policy in Cambodia.

One student was reported to have commented, "He wasn't really concerned why we were here." Another reported that Nixon was tired and had rambled on dully and aimlessly from subject to subject.

President Nixon was exhausted and under tremendous strain on that May weekend. As Bob Haldeman recorded in his diary for May 9, 1970, the president appeared to be holding up. Still, Haldeman expressed his apprehension about the future:

> I am concerned about his condition. The decision, the speech, the aftermath killings, riots, press, etc.; the press conference, the student confrontation have all taken their toll, and he has had very little sleep for a long time and his judgment, temper, and mood suffer badly as a result. On the other hand he has gone into a monumental crisis, fully recognized as such by the outside, and so far has come through extremely well. But there's a long way to go and he's in no condition to weather it. He's still riding on the crisis wave, but the letdown is near at hand and will be huge.

From the president's vantage point, his policy of Vietnamization of the war had been a success in the short run. However, by March of 1970 the United States was dropping 130,000 tons of bombs a month over North Vietnam. This was the greatest aerial bombardment in history—an area the size of Massachusetts was defoliated and made uninhabitable for animals and humans. Meanwhile, the peace talks in Paris dragged on and little was accomplished. Ambassador Henry Cabot Lodge resigned in frustration and, loyal to the last, blamed the Communists for the lack of progress, even though the United States had refused to offer Hanoi any concrete matching concessions. Thus, for the most part, the Nixon policy in Vietnam was an utter fraud.

Within two years, with the war still dragging on, President Nixon found himself in the midst of what should have been an easy campaign for reelection. However, H. R. Haldeman's dire apprehensions soon took on the appearance of prophecy. The letdown was near at hand and it was huge. It was to become known as Watergate.

8

WATERGATE I
Nixon, the Election of 1972, and the Break-in

> "I was determined that we should get to the bottom of the matter and that the truth should be fully brought out—no matter who was involved. . . . [the] responsibility therefore belongs here in this office, I accept it. . . . I want there to be no question remaining about the fact that the President has nothing to hide in this matter."

Like the assassination of John F. Kennedy, Watergate would be shrouded in mystery, complexity, and theories of conspiracy. A number of studies have even suggested that Richard Nixon was the victim, like President Kennedy before him, of a massive plot hatched deep within the government itself. These studies say that competing government agencies conspired and schemed to overthrow the Nixon presidency.

While conspiracy theories are interesting, the basic facts of the Watergate scandal contradict the conspiracy theorists. The trail of the affair and the attempt to cover it up eventually led to the White House and to the president himself. Although there is no real evidence to indicate that President Nixon was actually involved in (or even aware of) the attempted break-in and bugging of his rivals in the Democratic Party, it was the atmosphere in the Nixon White House, for which Nixon was responsible, that eventually set the stage for a seemingly petty crime and a massive criminal cover-up that involved White House staffers, members of the Nixon cabinet, and even the president himself.

The roots of Watergate were planted deep in the Nixon White House on that May weekend in 1970 when Nixon watched with dismay as the capital city—his capital city—was inundated with young people protesting their president's policies in Southeast Asia. In his mind, no matter what he did or said publicly, Nixon came to see the students and their allies as his enemies. Nixon's private memorandums to his staffers indicate that the president was overly preoccupied with those who dared oppose his policies. As his level of anxiety and anger grew, Nixon became convinced that his opponents were traitors—enemies of everything he held dear about America and Americans. He also began to see the media and even the Democratic Party in the same light as he saw the students—as enemies of his administration, and, thus, as enemies of the average, hard-working Americans Nixon dubbed "the silent majority."

Nixon's hostility to the media was expressed in almost every memo he sent to his closest aides. For example, in a taped memo to H. R. Haldeman on May 13, 1970, Nixon noted that the press was "out of tune with the people rather than the President." Nixon pointed out the media's bias against him. He told Haldeman that the White House's strategy should be to alienate the American people from the media:

> I think it is one [strategy] that can have considerable effect on the press and news media if they finally realize that they are losing their most important listener, viewer, and reader—the President of the United States—not because he personally objects to what they say about him because he doesn't, but because they have consistently opposed everything he stands for regardless of what the merits were.

The president's anxiety level heightened almost daily. On May 13, 1970, Nixon asked Haldeman to obtain information on the distribution of Department of Defense research funds to major colleges and universities. Nixon's stated purpose was to see if some $200 million of research money could be withheld from those universities that "play games with ROTC [Reserve Officers' Training Corps]." Afraid that Kissinger, an academic, might look askance at the government's blatant attempt to interfere with unrestricted university research, Nixon advised Haldeman to keep him out of the loop.

On May 14, Nixon instructed Haldeman to remove any consultants on the National Security Council (NSC) who were considered unfriendly by the administration. As Nixon said, "let's do a little housecleaning and sanitizing in this respect."

Nixon eventually became convinced that the antiwar movement was inspired by the Communists. By June of 1970 Nixon ordered the FBI, the CIA, and the National Security Agency (NSA) to mount a coordinated attack on "internal threats" to American security. Fortunately, FBI director J. Edgar Hoover refused to cooperate in this dangerous attempt to abridge basic American freedoms.

The Nixon administration also attempted to paint the Democratic Party as disloyal. In the congressional campaign of 1970, Jeb Stuart Magruder, an assistant to Haldeman, responded to his boss's request for a Republican strategy in the upcoming elections with the following suggestion: "The Democrats should be portrayed as being on the fringes: radical liberals who bus children, excuse disorders, tolerate crime, apologize for our wealth, and undercut the President's foreign policy."

By the spring of 1971 the Nixon administration had retreated into a dangerous fortress mentality. By that spring antiwar demonstrations had become a daily occurrence in Washington as some 15,000 demonstrators mobbed the capital city, dumping trash in the streets and bringing traffic to a halt. Over 12,000 arrests were made as the antiwar movement attempted to bring the Nixon government to a halt.

On June 13 the *New York Times* shook the administration further when it published the Pentagon Papers, a top-secret study of the Vietnam War commissioned by former secretary of defense Robert McNamara in 1967. Daniel Ellsberg, a brilliant young analyst who had worked for the Rand Corporation, a defense "think tank," had become disillusioned with the war and decided to leak the study to the *Times*. Publication of the Pentagon Papers revealed, for the first time, that the government had consistently lied to the American people about the war in Vietnam.

The Nixonites viewed publishing the documents as a traitorous betrayal of the nation by Ellsberg and his allies in the media, and they became obsessed with the idea of "leaks" within the administration. This growing paranoia had much to do with the atmosphere that created Watergate.

As the presidential election of 1972 drew near, the war in Vietnam still bedeviled the Nixon administration, obscuring other accomplishments in foreign affairs.

With the war dragging on, Vietnam now belonged to Nixon and his besieged administration, who still viewed it as one of the many pieces of the cold war puzzle. Both Nixon and Kissinger continued to see the looming specter of the Soviet Union, China, and the international Communist conspiracy behind many of their foreign policy problems. When the United States aided in the overthrow of the government in Chile headed by Marxist Salvador Allende, the Nixon government was only demonstrating the long-held mind-set that saw communism anywhere as a dangerous threat to the best interests of the American people. Although both Nixon and Kissinger publicly denied that the United States had any role in the whole affair (a military coup ousted Allende, who was then murdered), Kissinger's memoirs clearly hint at a high level of American involvement.

In February 1972, Nixon had traveled to the People's Republic of China, and that May he went to the Soviet Union. Fearful that U.S.-Chinese hostility had been aggravated because of Vietnam and the Taiwan issue (the U.S. was friendly toward the Chinese on Taiwan who opposed the Communist regime on the mainland), Nixon had asked Kissinger to begin secret negotiations to open the door a bit between the United States and China. As Kissinger noted in *The White House Years*, this initiative to China was fraught with political danger for Nixon. After all, Nixon was the man who had come to national attention as one of the most ardent anticommunists of his generation. As Kissinger wrote,

> Having made the decisions without executive or Congressional consultation, Nixon had left himself quite naked should anything go wrong; in such lonely decisions he was

Senator Edward M. Kennedy, the last Kennedy brother, who, but for Chappaquiddick, probably would have run against Richard Nixon in 1972. (Martin S. Goldman)

extremely courageous. But in his complicated personality high motives constantly warred with less lofty considerations. He was eager to be known as the first American leader to visit Peking.

The trip to Peking was a staged, televised extravaganza and was designed to have the maximum political impact at home as Nixon began to gear up for his 1972 reelection campaign. By elevating himself to the role of world statesman, Nixon hoped that he could easily ward off any criticism the Democrats might level against his failure to end the war in Vietnam.

That winter and spring, the Democratic Party's political disarray played right into the hands of the Republicans. The leading Democratic candidate for president, Senator Edward M. Kennedy of Massachusetts, had been eliminated as a presidential contender in the late summer of 1969. After attending a late-night party on the island of Chappaquiddick (off Martha's Vineyard), Kennedy left with a young woman, Mary Jo Kopechne. A few moments later, Kennedy's car plunged off a small bridge into a brackish pond. Instead of seeking help immediately, Kennedy left the scene of the accident. When the car was pulled out of the water the next day, Kopechne was dead. She had not drowned but had apparently been asphyxiated after hours without oxygen. In anticipation of a possible Kennedy challenge in 1972, the Nixon White House authorized a private investigator to travel to Martha's Vineyard and gather information about the accident. As reporter Leo Damore noted in *Senatorial Privilege*, "The major threat to Nixon's re-election had disappeared in a cloud of scandal so tainting the Kennedy mystique."

Other mysterious disasters for Democratic presidential contenders followed. Senator Edmund Muskie of Maine was dismissed as a candidate after breaking down in tears as he responded to a newspaper attack on his wife's reputation during the New Hampshire primary. George Wallace, who threatened to take many conservative votes from the Nixon column, was paralyzed by a would-be assassin's bullet and had to withdraw from the race. That left Hubert Humphrey and Senator George McGovern of South Dakota as the main contenders. With Humphrey still bearing the stigma of his service in the hated Johnson administration, Senator McGovern won several primaries and arrived at the Democratic convention in Miami that July as the front-runner. He received the nomination with 1,715 votes, but things began to go wrong almost immediately. The Democrats had allowed numerous speakers to present their views, and when McGovern finally rose to make his acceptance speech, it was 2:48 in the morning. Even in California, most viewers had gone to sleep. McGovern thus lost a golden chance to take his case before the American people, as his TV audience dwindled from 17,400,000 homes to 3,600,000.

In the following days McGovern suffered another reverse when the public learned that his choice for vice president, Senator Thomas Eagleton of Missouri, had been hospitalized three times for depression and had twice had electric shock therapy. In the media furor that ensued, McGovern appeared weak and wishy-washy. First, he announced that he was standing by Eagleton "1,000 percent . . . and I have no intention of dropping him from the ticket." Then he dropped Eagleton like a hot potato, offered the vice presidency to almost every major player in the party, and finally settled on R. Sargent Shriver, whose only political achievement was serving as head of the Peace Corps after being appointed by his brother-in-law, President John F. Kennedy.

To further compound McGovern's problems, it was revealed that he was secretly negotiating with Hanoi over ending the war in Vietnam. At first, he denied the charge. Then, after realizing that a lie would make him little different from the president he opposed, McGovern admitted to the endeavor, which he claimed was in the interest of peace. Thus, the Democratic nominee, a thoroughly decent man if not much of a politician, was mortally wounded before the fall campaign had even begun.

From the White House viewpoint, it looked like clear sailing for Nixon's reelection—except for one event, which seemed insignificant at the time. Early on the morning of June 17, 1972, at 2:30 A.M., five men dressed in business suits had been arrested for breaking into the headquarters of the Democratic National Committee in the exclusive Watergate office-apartment-hotel complex in downtown Washington. The men had been detected by Frank Wills, an observant security guard, who then alerted the District of Columbia police. The men all wore surgical gloves, and the police confiscated a walkie-talkie, 40 rolls of unexposed film, two 35-millimeter cameras, lock picks, pen-sized tear gas guns, and electronic bugging devices. Curiously, the men were all carrying large amounts of cash, mainly in $100 bills with sequential serial numbers.

The arrested Watergate burglars had rather impressive credentials. One was James A. McCord, a former CIA employee, who was working for the Committee to Re-elect the President (CREEP) and the Republican National Committee as security coordinator. The other four men—Bernard L. Barker, Virgilio R. Gonzalez, Eugenio R. Martinez, and Frank A. Sturgis—were anti-Castro Cubans from Miami with ties to the CIA. There were others who had not been caught but who had been in the Watergate illegally at the time of the break-in: G. Gordon Liddy, a former FBI agent who actually served in the Nixon White House on the staff of the President's Domestic Council (a lawyer, he came to CREEP in 1971 as general counsel); and E. Howard Hunt, a former CIA operative and prolific author of spy novels who was head of security for CREEP. The police found Hunt's name and number in the address book of one of the burglars with the small notations "W. House" and

"W.H." The police leaked the information to the *Washington Post*. Bob Woodward, a young *Post* reporter on the metropolitan desk, was working on the break-in as a local crime story. Woodward called the White House to find out if Hunt was still on the payroll. A clerk told him that Hunt was on the staff of Charles Colson, a special counsel to the president who was known around the Nixon White House as a "hatchet man." Woodward then called Colson's office at the White House and was told that Hunt worked as a writer for the Washington public relations firm Robert R. Mullen and Company. Then Woodward called Mullen and got Hunt on the phone. Woodward asked Hunt why his name and phone number were in the address books of two of the Watergate burglars. "Good God!" Hunt responded. Then he said, "In view that the matter is under adjudication, I have no comment" and hung up. Although he was still inexperienced as a journalist, Woodward smelled a story and alerted Carl Bernstein, one of the paper's two Virginia political reporters, who also had been working on the Watergate story. Eventually, the investigative team of Woodward and Bernstein dug out more of the story than any other reporters working on the case and brought the truth of Watergate to the American people.

At the time of the break-in, President Nixon was vacationing in the Bahamas. The following day, June 18, he arrived back in Key Biscayne, Florida, with his friend Bebe Rebozo. In the Sunday edition of the *Miami Herald* Nixon read a small story on the front page headlined, "MIAMIANS HELD IN D.C. TRY TO BUG DEMO HEADQUARTERS." According to Nixon, he called Haldeman, discussed a number of issues but did not mention the Watergate story. Then the president took a long swim in the ocean. As he later recalled,

> My reaction to the Watergate break-in was completely pragmatic. If it was also cynical, it was a cynicism born of experience. I had been in politics too long, and seen everything from dirty tricks to vote fraud. I could not muster much moral outrage over a political bugging.

The roots of Watergate can be found in the creation of the so-called "plumbers"—a special investigations unit established back in 1971 in the White House. The plumbers unit was the brainchild of Tom Charles Huston, a young White House aide who, with the president's approval and authority, authorized the FBI, CIA, and other intelligence agencies to violate basic American civil liberties in pursuit of information on antiwar activities and leaks of classified information from the White House and other federal agencies. These violations included the interception of cables or private correspondence (including domestic mail) and the searching of private homes without a warrant.

Huston's creation of what Theodore H. White has labeled the "super police" led to the formation of the plumbers. The group even had a White House office with the sign PLUMBERS on the door. Headed by presidential adviser Charles Colson, the plumbers engaged in a broad range of activities—most of them illegal—to deal with leaks of information. Increasingly angry and frustrated over White House leaks, the president had said, "If we can't get anyone in this damn government to do something serious about the problem [leaks] that may be the most serious one we have, then, by God, we'll do it ourselves." As early as 1969 Nixon had ordered John Ehrlichman to set up "a little group right here in the White House. Have them get off their tails and find out what's going on and figure out how to stop it." As Ehrlichman observed in his memoir *Witness to Power: The Nixon Years*, written after he went to prison, the problem in the Nixon administration was that the president didn't confide everything he was doing to any one person and that even Nixon's closest aides were sometimes kept out of the presidential loop. "Most of us," Ehrlichman wrote, "operated in watertight compartments, unaware of what Nixon was ordering our colleagues to do."

The plumbers had recruited E. Howard Hunt and G. Gordon Liddy to deal with clandestine operations, which included a break-in at the office of Dr. Lewis Fielding, Daniel Ellsberg's psychiatrist. Incredibly, both Hunt and Liddy had offices in the White House. Thus, with criminal operations being hatched right in the White House, the stage was set for what happened in the Watergate complex in June 1972.

When it was clear, by the spring of 1972, that Attorney General John Mitchell was going to step down from his post to head the Committee to Re-elect the President, Liddy visited

Hunt in his office in the Executive Office Building (part of the White House complex). Liddy had some interesting news for his friend:

> [John] Dean [the President's counsel] told me the AG [Attorney General John Mitchell] wants me to become general counsel for the Committee to Re-elect the President! . . . But here's the most important thing—get this: The AG wants me to set up an intelligence organization for the campaign. It'll be big, Howard, and important. They don't want a repetition of the last campaign; this time they want to know everything that's going on. Everything.

Liddy then told Hunt that Dean had promised there would be "plenty of money available—half a million for openers and there's more where that came from. A lot more. . . . What I want to know is, can I count on you? Will you help me?" A few months later, at a White House reception for opera star Beverly Sills, Hunt and his wife Dorothy passed through a receiving line where they were greeted by President Nixon and the first lady. "I'm working with Chuck Colson now, Mr. President," Hunt said. "Oh, yes," Nixon replied with a smile, "I know about that."

Did President Nixon really know what Hunt was doing in the White House? Should he have known? More important, did Nixon know what was being planned when John Mitchell took over the reins at CREEP and brought Hunt and Liddy onto the staff? In his memoirs, Nixon says,

> . . . my confidence in the CRP was undermined more by the stupidity of the DNC bugging attempt than by its illegality. The whole thing made so little sense. Why? I wondered. Why then? Why in such a blundering way? And, why, of all places, the Democratic National Committee? Anyone who knew anything about politics would know that a national committee headquarters was a useless place to go for inside information on a presidential campaign.

On June 20, 1972, the *Washington Post* reported that Howard Hunt was tied to the Watergate break-in and that Hunt had worked for Charles Colson at the White House. The president was unnerved. He later recalled,

The mention of Colson's name gave me a start. It was one thing if the CRP was involved, or even a former low-level White House staff member like Hunt. But Colson was a member of my inner circle of aides and advisers, and if he was drawn in it was a whole new situation. I had always valued his hardball instincts. Now I wondered if he might have gone too far.

President Nixon had other problems as well. The arrest of the Watergate burglars had generated furious activity among his staff as incriminating documents were shredded and E. Howard Hunt's name was removed from the White House telephone directory. In addition, tens of thousands of dollars in cash (mostly in $100 bills) were taken from White House safes to keep the Watergate burglars quiet and to keep them from revealing the names of the men who had hired them. To add to Nixon's woes, the Democratic National Committee had filed a damage suit against CREEP and the five burglars for invasion of privacy. And George McGovern, the Democratic candidate, was beginning to ask questions about who had authorized the Watergate break-in as he campaigned around the country.

From the beginning of his presidency Richard Nixon had made plans for his reelection. He had been determined that he would not risk his reelection chances because of a lack of available cash. Consequently, large donations, both legal and illegal, had flowed into the Nixon campaign coffers. By April 7, 1972, Nixon had raised over $20 million, some $1.8 million of it in cash that was kept in safes and deposit boxes in the White House and in the CREEP offices on K Street. Campaign treasurer Hugh Sloan later recalled that over $6 million had come into the campaign over a two-day period. Thus, there was plenty of money available to pay off the Watergate burglars and anyone else who might need "hush money." President Nixon would ultimately authorize payments of more than $460,000 to keep Hunt, Liddy, and the other Watergate defendants from bringing the crime to the very gates of the White House.

Nixon began to proceed on a number of tracks in his attempt to contain the fallout from the burgeoning Watergate problem. In the early months he was successful. He ordered his chief of staff, H. R. Haldeman, to try to discourage the investigation of Watergate by the FBI, on the spurious grounds of national security.

At the same time, while John Dean, the young White House counsel, was ostensibly conducting a "complete investigation" of Watergate at the president's behest, he was busy covering up the crimes himself. Dean gathered sensitive materials from Howard Hunt's White House safe and tossed them into the Potomac River; he coached potential witnesses; and he met secretly with acting FBI director L. Patrick Gray to find out how far the FBI's own investigation was progressing. This blatantly criminal violation of the federal investigatory process was becoming standard operating procedure at the White House.

As Dean recalled after his own conviction,

> I sustained the image of myself as "counsel" rather than an active participant for as long as I could, but the line blurred and finally vanished. I was too central a figure, and there was too much hasty activity required as the cover-up proceeded speedily along its two main themes—containing the Justice Department investigation, and paying the hush money to the defendants. I am still not sure when I crossed the line into criminal culpability.

At this point, most Americans cared little about Watergate. As far as the public was concerned, Watergate was just what the president's press secretary, Ron Ziegler, said it was: "a third-rate burglary." Few journalists, other than the intrepid Woodward and Bernstein, were seriously exercised over a bunch of bungling burglars who seemed more like the Three Stooges than like subverters of the American democratic process. After the election, George McGovern was to complain bitterly that the press never laid a glove on Nixon. As McGovern said, "Not a single reporter could gather the courage to ask a question about the bugging and burglary of the Democratic National Committee."

On November 7, 1972, more Americans voted than ever before in history. Of 77,681,461 votes, Nixon had 47,167,319 to McGovern's 29,168,509—the largest numerical margin in American history. Of the 50 states, Nixon took 49. He lost only in liberal Massachusetts and the District of Columbia. It was a landslide of historic proportions.

There was, however, a great irony in Nixon's triumphant reelection. He had campaigned in 1972, as he had in the past, against concentrating power in Washington and against giving too much authority to the president. As Theodore H. White observed,

> He was for returning home power to the people in their communities. But in practice he took to himself more personal power, delegated to more individuals of his staff the use or abuse of that power, than any other President of modern times.

Instead of being overjoyed at his landslide victory, Nixon was vaguely uneasy, oddly sullen, and somewhat melancholy on the day after his greatest triumph. Physically, he was suffering from a painful toothache. One cabinet member reported a very difficult meeting in which the president hinted that he wanted everyone's resignations and that he wasn't about to allow himself to go downhill during the all-important second term. As the cabinet official noted, "There was this joyless, brooding quality as he talked, you almost had the impression he had lost. . . . There was this foreboding in the way he spoke."

Looking back on that moment in his memoirs, Richard Nixon makes it clear that he was not a happy man. Nixon himself pondered his inability to savor his landslide win:

> I am at a loss to explain the melancholy that settled over me on that victorious night. Perhaps it was caused by the painful tooth. To some extent the marring effects of Watergate may have played a part.

Clearly, Watergate was never very far from Richard Nixon's mind.

9

WATERGATE II
From Cover-up to Disgrace

"In all my years of public life, I have never obstructed justice. And I think too, that I could say that in my years of public life, that I welcome this kind of examination, because people have got to know whether or not their President is a crook. Well, I am not a crook."

On a cold and blustery Washington day, January 20, 1973, Richard Nixon was sworn in for his second term. He wanted his second inaugural address to be inspirational. His conclusion turned out to be eerily prophetic: "We shall answer to God, to history, and to our conscience for the way in which we use these years."

Peace was still eluding Nixon in Vietnam, the Democratic 93rd Congress was hostile to his domestic program, and there was even talk of holding up funds for the continued conduct of the war. The CIA and FBI were refusing to cooperate with the Watergate cover-up—indeed, the FBI investigation pressed on, with daily leaks to the press. Thus, despite his overwhelming mandate, Richard Nixon had big problems with the Democrats, the media, and the Washington bureaucracy he had always detested. In addition, the

Secretary of State Henry Kissinger, appointed by President Nixon, dances with Imelda Marcos, wife of the president of the Philippines. (Times Books, Promo Photo)

courts were going to continue to pursue Watergate no matter where it happened to lead.

On the positive side, Nixon had halted the bombing of North Vietnam on January 15 in anticipation of a negotiated treaty to end the war. On January 27, Nixon's long-sought goal was finally achieved. After seemingly endless negotiations in Paris, where arguments with the North Vietnamese over trivial matters held up the process for months, Henry Kissinger and his staff finally hammered out the details of an agreement. After they secured the approval of South Vietnam's president Nguyen Van Thieu, a cease-fire went into effect. Although the agreement eventually fell apart, with South Vietnam falling to the Communists, Kissinger was convinced "that the agreement could have worked." As he later wrote,

> We had no illusions about Hanoi's long-term goals. Nor did we go through the agony of four years of war and searing negotiations simply to achieve a "decent interval" for our withdrawal. We were determined to do our utmost to enable Saigon to grow in security and prosperity so that it could prevail in any political struggle. We sought not an interval before collapse, but lasting peace with honor. But for the collapse of executive authority as a result of Watergate, I believe we would have succeeded.

If the possibility of peace in Vietnam was the good news in the Nixon administration, Watergate continued to be bad news in 1973. The press (especially the *Washington Post*, the *New York Times*, and the *Miami Herald*), special prosecutors, federal judges, and members of Congress began to focus their attention on the nagging and unanswered questions surrounding Watergate.

Once the usually docile American public awoke to the dangerous implications of Watergate, aroused by the increasing media attention, the president's situation rapidly deteriorated. The tragedy is that, in his increasing isolation, Nixon did not know it or would not believe it. The trouble began in the spring of 1973 when United States District Court Judge John Sirica, a Republican appointee who was not dissatisfied with the Nixon presidency, angrily accepted the guilty pleas of the four Cubans. Sirica posited a simple question before leveling his sentence: "Why did you break into the Watergate?" he asked. "It pertained to the Cuban situation . . ." Eugenio Martinez answered. Sirica rolled his eyes in abject disbelief, and the men were taken off to jail. Three days before the sentencing, James McCord, the only non-Cuban of the original burglars, sent a letter to Judge Sirica. Worried about his family, threats to his life, and the possibility of a stiff sentence for the break-in, McCord told Sirica that pressure had been applied to keep the Watergate defendants silent, that perjury had occurred in the trial, and that there were others involved who had not been identified in court testimony. McCord told Sirica that Watergate was not a CIA operation, as the White House had been putting out for public consumption, but that it did involve other officials in the government. As Sirica said to his clerk, "This is going to break this case wide open." For

John Dean, who worried from inside the White House, "The dam was cracking."

News of the McCord letter had filtered back to the president and his closest advisers, who huddled for a number of long strategy sessions on March 21, 1973. At a morning meeting that lasted a little under two hours, the president met with Haldeman and Dean. Dean was now aware that he too had crossed the line of legality, and he was worried that he was now culpable in the attempt to cover up the crime of Watergate. Expressing those fears to Nixon, Dean said, "I have the impression that you don't know everything I know and it makes it very difficult for you to make judgments." Then, in what was to become one of the most widely discussed exchanges between the president and his counsel, Dean said,

> We have a cancer within, close to the Presidency, that is growing. It is growing daily. It's compounded, growing geometrically now, because it compounds itself.

He told Nixon that the administration was being blackmailed and that people would have to start perjuring themselves. For the most part, the president did not respond to Dean's anxieties. The conversation continued and Dean began to discuss his "theory of containment"—how to keep Watergate under control. To that the president responded with one word, "Sure." Does that mean at this point that Nixon knew and approved of the cover-up? It appears that way, but later Nixon would argue strongly that this was not the case. Dean continued and said, "To try to hold it right where it was." Nixon seemed to approve and responded, "Right."

Then Dean moved toward the bottom line of his meeting with the president: the problem of hush money and the demands being made by E. Howard Hunt, who by that time had been indicted. Instead of rising up in righteous indignation and tossing his counsel out of the Oval Office for daring to discuss bribery and obstruction of justice, Nixon responded with a question: "How much money do you need?" "I would say," Dean answered, "these people are going to cost a million dollars over the next two years." Nixon's reply is absolutely shocking. The president said,

> We could get that. On the money, if you need the money you could get that. You could get a million dollars. You could get it in cash. I know where it could be gotten. It is not easy, but it could be done. But the question is who the hell would handle it? Any ideas on that?

At another point in the meeting Dean advised Nixon, "If this ever blows, then we are in a cover-up situation. I think it would be extremely damaging to you." Later in the conversation Nixon rejected the notion of a cover-up. But his rejection seemed oblique and disconnected from the other segments of the meeting. The men also discussed the option of using national security as grounds to block any further investigation.

What did these conversations mean? Theodore H. White writes, "It is impossible to misinterpret the flow of conversation: the president has ordered Dean to buy time for him." Later that night, after telephone calls between former attorney general John Mitchell, Dean, Haldeman, and Fred LaRue, the deputy director of CREEP, $75,000 was passed on to E. Howard Hunt through his attorney. Thus, it also appeared that the president was sanctioning the crime of bribery.

Now the genie was out of the bottle and events began to move so rapidly that no one could possibly have contained the situation. The Senate formed a Select Committee on Campaign Practices, chaired by the crusty senator from North Carolina, Sam Ervin. On March 26, James McCord testified before the committee in executive session. Within 24 hours the *Los Angeles Times* was reporting that McCord had implicated John Dean and Jeb Magruder. Magruder was a link to the former attorney general, and Dean was, of course, a link right to the top of the White House. The other major newspapers had the story plastered on their front pages by the next day.

By April 1973 the noose seemed to be rapidly tightening around the Nixon administration's neck. On April 27 the acting director of the FBI, L. Patrick Gray, whose nomination for director had already been withdrawn by Nixon, resigned after the *New York Times* revealed that Ehrlichman and Dean had confiscated incriminating documents from Howard Hunt's White House safe on June 28, 1972, and given them to Gray. Gray stored the papers at his house and, claiming never to have examined them, burned them. In addition to his obstruction of justice, Gray was also facing a possible perjury charge, having testified to the Senate Judiciary Committee that Dean made no effort to conceal Hunt's papers. The president heard the news while flying on Air Force One and ordered Ehrlichman to demand Gray's immediate resignation.

The next in line to fall at the White House were Haldeman and Ehrlichman. Haldeman was desperately worried that Magruder would break under pressure from the prosecutors. Nixon worried about Dean, and he had asked Ehrlichman to keep Dean on track. By this time it was known that Dean had hired his own lawyer, who began talking to federal prosecutors after April 5. Clearly, the inner circle of the Watergate cover-up had been breached.

Nixon expressed apprehension to Haldeman that Dean had secretly tape-recorded their conversation of March 21. But Haldeman was now worried about his own skin and cared little about his president's anxieties over tapes.

By late April Washington was awash in gossip, rumor, and innuendo. President Nixon decided that his two most trusted aides had been compromised and had to resign. He said, "The attacks on them had destroyed their ability to serve in their high positions."

On Sunday, April 29, Nixon summoned Haldeman and Ehrlichman to Camp David, the presidential retreat in the Maryland mountains. Both men, of course, knew that they were about to be fired. Ehrlichman was angry and had difficulty understanding why, after being such a good soldier, he was being asked to fall on his sword. Haldeman disagreed with Nixon's decision but outwardly appeared more resigned to his fate. Nixon called them in one at a time for the emotional farewell. Haldeman was first. Haldeman, who tried to appear loyal and supportive, recalled that Nixon "was in terrible shape." In his diary, Haldeman wrote,

> He [Nixon] said he's thought it all through, and that he was the one that started Colson on his projects, he was the one who told Dean to cover up, he was the one who made Mitchell Attorney General, and later his campaign manager, and so on. And that he now has to face that and live with it, and that for that reason, after he gets other things completed, that he too will probably have to resign. He never said that directly, but implied it.

Then Ehrlichman's turn came. "You'll have to resign," the president said. "You've been my conscience all through this mess. You were right about a lot of things—you were right about Colson and you were right about Mitchell. It's like cutting off my arms. You and Bob. You'll need money. I have some—Bebe has it—and you can have it." Ehrlichman shook his head sadly. Tears were welling up in his eyes. "That would just make things worse," Ehrlichman said. "You can do one thing for me, though, sometime.... Just explain all this to my kids will you?" Then Ehrlichman left, wiping his eyes with his handkerchief.

On April 30 the president went on nationwide television to announce the resignations and to formally address the Watergate issue for the first time. In a highly emotional speech in which he was not at his best, he announced "one of the most difficult decisions of my presidency," the resignations of Haldeman and Ehrlichman. He called his aides "two of the finest public servants it has been my privilege to know." Then Nixon added that their resignations were not to be interpreted as an indication of any personal wrongdoing on their parts but rather came as a result of the rumors and accusations that were swirling around the Watergate investigations.

Nixon pledged that he would seek out the facts of Watergate and then take appropriate action. "There can be no whitewash at the White House," the president said. He also announced the appointment of Elliott Richardson, a prominent Massachusetts Republican, as attorney general, and of Leonard Garment as the new White House counsel, replacing John Dean.

It seems clear, in retrospect, that Nixon still didn't appear to understand the precariousness of his situation.

Even years later, when he wrote his *Memoirs*, Nixon still didn't understand that his own lies to the American people proved, in the end, to be his undoing. As Nixon wrote,

> I believe that a totally honest answer would have been neither a simple yes or no.
> If I had given the true answer, I would have had to say that without fully realizing the implications of my actions I had become deeply entangled in the complicated mesh of decisions, inactions, misunderstandings, and conflicting motivations that comprised the Watergate coverup; I

would have had to admit that I still did not know the whole story and therefore did not know the full extent of my involvement in it; and I would have had to give the damaging specifics of what I did know while leaving open the possibility that much more might come out later.

In May and June the Senate Select Committee began televised hearings on Watergate that riveted the nation. The witnesses included John Dean, who gave a 245-page opening statement and provided days of testimony in which he acknowledged his role in the White House cover-up. Dean's memory appeared to be remarkable. He related in exhaustive detail his involvement in the cover-up as far back as June 1972, when he met with Herbert Kalmbach, Richard Nixon's personal attorney, in the Mayflower Hotel to discuss payment of hush money.

Assessing Dean's meticulous testimony, many public officials were becoming increasingly convinced that there was something terribly and dramatically wrong within the Nixon White House. William Ruckelshaus, the newly appointed director of the FBI, believed Dean had been truthful. As Ruckelshaus said, "On a credibility scale of one to ten Dean was an eight. He was pretty credible, he had a remarkable memory."

If Dean's testimony was shocking, the testimony of Alexander Butterfield, a Haldeman aide who was deputy assistant to the president, was a bombshell that almost blew the committee members out of their seats. When minority counsel Fred Thompson asked Butterfield if he was aware of any listening devices in the president's office, Butterfield's answer froze the entire nation. Butterfield answered, "I was aware of listening devices, yes sir." Thompson pressed and Butterfield then disclosed that President Nixon had taping devices installed in the Executive Office Building as well as in the Oval Office. For the first time, the American people became aware that whatever Nixon had or had not done in regard to Watergate was on the record. But would Nixon release the tapes? It appeared that he would do everything he could to avoid this possibility as Nixon quickly moved to thwart the committee's attempts to hear the tapes. On July 16, Nixon instructed that no Secret Service agents could testify regarding their White House duties, which had included installation of the taping devices. Nixon also sent committee chair Sam Ervin a letter barring any access to the tapes. With the president obviously "stonewalling," on July 23 the Senate committee voted unanimously to issue a subpoena for the tapes. Nixon rejected the subpoena.

At the end of July, after a bout with viral pneumonia, Nixon left the Bethesda Naval Hospital to return to the White House. A small group of White House workers gathered in the Rose Garden to greet their returning boss. Nixon spoke movingly of the little time that was left for him to finish his tasks. He pointed out that there were those who wanted him to resign but that was just "plain poppycock." He would go on. "Let others wallow in Watergate," he said, "we are going to do our job."

That fall, Archibald Cox, a professor of law at Harvard Law School who had been appointed to the new position of Watergate special prosecutor, sought to obtain the tapes through a court order. Cox was supported in his efforts by Attorney General Elliott Richardson and FBI director William Ruckelshaus. When Nixon ordered Ruckelshaus to fire Cox, he refused. Nixon then fired Ruckelshaus, forced Richardson to resign, and got Solicitor General Robert Bork, the second-ranking official in the Department of Justice, to fire Cox. Once again, Nixon drastically miscalculated the reaction of the American people. As Cox later recalled, "The public reaction against President Nixon . . . was so great that the president was forced to change his position and send his lawyer to court to say he would comply with the order."

Indeed, Nixon's actions had inspired a national frenzy of public reaction. His new chief of staff, General Alexander Haig, was to call Saturday, October 20, 1973, "the day of the firestorm." The press was to dub it "the Saturday night massacre." As Theodore H. White noted, "The reaction that evening was as near instantaneous as it had been at Pearl Harbor, or the day of John F. Kennedy's assassination—an explosion as unpredictable and as sweeping as mass hysteria."

Outside the White House crowds of angry protesters gathered. They held up signs that read, "HONK FOR IMPEACHMENT." One man, in a Nixon mask, was dressed in a striped prison suit.

The news departments of NBC and CBS prepared 90-minute television specials that only served to further enflame public opinion. John Chancellor, who anchored the "NBC Nightly News," breathlessly appeared on his evening newscast and used the word "unbelievable" to introduce the day's events. One by one, the press chimed in, either reporting or editorializing on the firings. Longtime Nixon friends in the print media began to desert the president. The *Baltimore Sun*, a staunch supporter of Nixon's reelection in 1972, declared that Nixon had "lost touch with truth and principle." And *Time* magazine, in the first editorial in its history, declared, "The President Should Resign." Theodore H. White accurately observed, "The question was now not one of burglary, break-in, cover-up, but of power itself—and the White House had been caught in a total misreading of the American mind."

The Watergate scandal now became a struggle between Nixon and the American people. The people wanted to hear what their president had said behind closed doors in their White House. They wanted to know if their president had misused his power, had undermined the Constitution, and was a liar or, even worse, a criminal.

As if Nixon didn't have enough troubles that fall, two other crises pressed down on the beleaguered president. On October 6, the Yom Kippur War broke out in the Middle East when Egypt and Syria attacked Israel. Worried that the Arabs had been encouraged by the Soviets, Nixon watched with dismay as the surprised Israelis suffered significant losses. To his credit, Nixon overcame strong opposition from the Joint Chiefs of Staff and ordered that the Israelis be quickly resupplied to avoid total disaster. This action enabled the Israelis to recover and take the battle to their enemies. When the Israelis were within striking distance of Damascus and Cairo the United States persuaded them to halt the attack, thus ensuring a stalemate. This eventually led to peace talks that culminated in the historic Camp David Accords of 1978. Israeli prime minister Golda Meir remained grateful to Nixon and later observed that "he did not break a single one of the promises he made to us."

Closer to home, Nixon's vice president, Spiro T. Agnew, had been under investigation for taking bribes and kickbacks while governor of Maryland. On October 10, protesting his innocence, Agnew pleaded nolo contendere (no contest) to charges of income tax evasion and accepting bribes. In return he received a suspended sentence and a fine of $10,000. Several hours earlier, Agnew had tendered his resignation to Nixon through the secretary of state. Agnew's resignation was bad news for the embattled Nixon in more ways than one. As historian Stanley I. Kutler points out, "Agnew had one special contribution to make to the Watergate saga: his forced resignation removed a significant obstacle to unseating the President of the United States. Agnew's presence as Nixon's constitutional successor acted as a brake on impeachment."

Utilizing the Twenty-fifth Amendment to the Constitution proposed by Congress in the wake of the Kennedy assassination and adopted in 1967, Nixon replaced Agnew with Michigan congressman Gerald R. Ford. The new vice president, who had been House minority leader, was well liked on Capitol Hill and was known as a good and decent man by both Democrats and Republicans.

If Nixon thought that the "Saturday night massacre" of Archibald Cox had solved his problems over the special prosecutor, he was sadly mistaken. The new special prosecutor, Leon Jaworski, was a Houston lawyer with strong ties to Lyndon Johnson. Chosen by the White House and Robert Bork, with assurances from Bork that there would be no restraints on him to pursue any presidential documents, including the tapes, Jaworski came to Washington convinced that the president could not have had any criminal culpability in Watergate. But the Jaworski appointment was a big loss for Nixon, who had finally had to cave in to the public outcry for a special prosecutor possessing complete independence.

Jaworski was appointed on November 1, and from that time on there ensued a legal tug of war between his office and the White House for the Nixon tapes. Aware that he was bound to lose in the courts, the president sought a compromise solution. He began to indicate to friendly congressmen that he might cooperate by releasing "summaries" of what appeared on the tapes. In a strong counteroffensive, Nixon took to the airwaves and then met with 241 Republican and 46 Democratic senators and congressmen in what *Newsweek* magazine cynically dubbed "Operation Candor." But none of it worked. With the Senate committee still issuing subpoenas for additional presidential materials, Nixon tried to hold them off by arguing that the confidentiality of the executive office must be protected against invasions by other branches of the government. However, in order to avoid being held in contempt of court, Nixon partially complied with an order from Judge Sirica on November 26 and had his aides surrender seven tapes. On one of them, a crucial Haldeman-Nixon conversation on June 20, 1972, there was an 18½-minute gap that the president blamed on his personal secretary, Rose Mary Woods. According to Nixon, Woods told him that she had reached for a telephone while transcribing the tape and had mistakenly hit the wrong button for "about four or five minutes." The press and many cartoonists had a field day with this news. *Washington Post* cartoonist Herblock drew a contorted Rose Mary Woods being carried into an emergency room on a stretcher with the caption, "SHE TRIED PUSHING A TAPE RECORDER BUTTON WHILE HOLDING HER FOOT ON A PEDAL AND REACHING BACK FOR A TELEPHONE."

On December 21 Jaworski, who had been given access to some of the tapes by Judge Sirica, met with Alexander Haig in the White House. Their discussion focused on Nixon's March 21 meeting with John Dean, which Haig described as "terrible beyond description." Jaworski agreed, calling it "unbelievable." Still, Haig insisted that White House lawyers felt Nixon had done nothing criminal. Jaworski disagreed and advised that the president hire himself a good criminal lawyer. Jaworski was appalled by the stupidity of taping private conversations in the face of "an evil approach and wrongful conduct by the President."

By the end of the year, Richard Nixon, more than anyone around him, finally seemed to understand the impossibility of his own position. On December 23, while visiting Camp David for Christmas, he began to make some notes. Across the top of the page, Nixon scrawled, "Last Christmas here."

On April 29, 1974, exhausted by the ongoing demands made by the Senate Select Committee and the special prosecutor and now facing the real possibility of the first impeachment hearings by the House Judiciary Committee since the presidency of Andrew Johnson following the Civil War, Nixon relented. He had his staff clean up the tapes as best they could—Ron Ziegler's press aide Diane Sawyer was instructed to remove as many obscenities from the president's language as possible—and release the transcripts of the tapes. That night President Nixon went on national radio and television and, in a long address to the American people, continued to claim his innocence by offering up more than 1,200 pages of his private conversations between September 15, 1972, and April 27, 1973. "I want," Nixon said, "there to be no question remaining about the fact that the President has nothing to hide in this matter. The impeachment of the President is a remedy of last resort. It is the most solemn act of our entire constitutional process."

The presidential transcripts became an immediate bestseller. They showed the dark and sleazy side of Richard Nixon, a side that he had been able to keep hidden from the American people throughout his public life. Even cleaned up, with references to Jesus Christ deleted, words like "damn" replacing "god damn," and "expletive deleted" in place of crude obscenities, the Nixon transcripts were a shocking window into the mind of one of the strangest men ever to inhabit the White House. Even Nixon's friends were appalled by the shoddy nature of his conduct in the highest office in the land. Columnist Joseph Alsop described the atmosphere in the Nixon White House as "the back room of a second-rate advertising agency in a suburb of hell." And *New York Times* columnist William Safire, a one-time Nixon speechwriter, said his former boss was "guilty of conduct unbecoming a President." Once again Richard Nixon had drastically miscalculated. Instead of silencing his growing legion of critics and driving the wolves from the White House door, publication of *The White House Transcripts* had just the opposite effect. Editorial and public opinion lined up all over the country against the president. The only thing Nixon seemed to have going for him was the fact that the tapes provided no "smoking gun"—no real evidence that the president had committed any irrefutable crime that could lead to his impeachment and removal.

There are some Watergate scholars who argue that there already was a "smoking gun." They summarize their argument by citing the Supreme Court case of *U.S. v. U.S. District Court for the Eastern District of Michigan*, a decision that the Court handed down just two days after the Watergate break-in in June 1972. The argument goes that Nixon had already violated the U.S. Constitution as a result of his role in officially sanctioning breaking of the law by the federal government. In this case, Nixon was seeking to have the Court officially approve of his administration's illegal projects. Arthur Kinoy, the lawyer who argued against the Nixon administration position in this case before the Supreme Court, has written,

Nixon was seeking a stamp of legitimacy for a sweeping strategy of governmental lawlessness—for the suspension, if not the abandonment, of the elementary forms of constitutional protection. . . . what was at stake here was a bid to establish a legal "cover" to sanction wholesale experimentation with the abandonment of constitutional government.

The Supreme Court, in its wisdom, voted 8–0 (with Nixon appointee Justice William Rehnquist abstaining) to halt the expansion of executive power that would ultimately have legalized everything—including the Watergate break-in, the Huston plan, and the burglary at the office of Daniel Ellsberg's psychiatrist. As Kinoy noted, "The Court's decision that Monday morning left the administration in total disarray."

Kinoy hypothesizes that the Watergate break-in might have been directly related to the Court's 8–0 decision (as a result of a leak or even the bugging of the Supreme Court, he suggests that the Watergate burglars may have been dismantling bugs from a previous break-in). However, Kinoy offers little in the way of evidence beyond mere supposition to back up his version of a "smoking gun" held in the president's hands—that is, the attempt to subvert the Constitution.

Smoking gun or no, the House Judiciary Committee met on May 9 to consider resolutions of impeachment. On May 15 the committee issued subpoenas for more tapes. On May 30 the committee's chair, Congressman Peter Rodino of New Jersey, refused to compromise by accepting written statements and even rejected the offer of a private session where the president would be examined under oath. The House alone, Rodino maintained, had the power to conduct an investigation and determine the relevant evidence, not the person under scrutiny.

Nixon and his attorney, James St. Clair, argued that the tapes were still protected under the principle of executive privilege and that they belonged to Nixon. The struggle over the tapes soon erupted into a constitutional contest. On July 8, 1974, Special Prosecutor Jaworski and presidential attorney St. Clair argued their case before the Supreme Court of the United States.

Throughout July, the news for Nixon was all bad. On July 12 the president was informed while flying on Air Force One that

John Ehrlichman had been convicted of perjury and conspiracy to violate the rights of Daniel Ellsberg's psychiatrist. Nixon recalled, "I was deeply depressed by the tragic irony of this development. Ellsberg, who had leaked top-secret documents, had gone free. Ehrlichman, who was trying to prevent such leaks, had been convicted." Then, on the morning of July 23, the day before the House Judiciary Committee had scheduled televised hearings, Nixon learned that a number of conservative Republicans on the committee were jumping ship in favor of impeachment. With his options reduced to resignation or impeachment, Nixon once again considered resignation. In Nixon's recollection, this was his "Lowest point in the presidency, and Supreme Court still to come."

Nixon's pessimism was justified. On July 24 the Supreme Court ruled 8–0 (Justice Rehnquist, who had served in the Nixon Justice Department, recused himself) that Nixon would have to turn over the materials under subpoena. Nixon later said, "This decision in the case of the United States v. Nixon was widely heralded as one of the Court's finest hours . . . I thought that the United States had lost. I felt that the presidency itself was a casualty of this ruling."

The American public barely had time to catch its breath from the decision. On that same evening, the televised House Judiciary proceedings on the impeachment of the president got underway. Passionate statements about the rule of law and government ethics were read into the public record by stalwart young representatives like Maine Republican William Cohen and Democrat Barbara Jordan of Texas. Cohen had prepared for the hearings by reading the *Federalist Papers*, the classic statement of the principles of American government written in 1787. He wondered, "How in the world did we ever get from the *Federalist Papers* to the edited transcripts?" Cohen concluded that the president's wounds had been self-inflicted and that Nixon had used the excuse of "executive privilege" for all the wrong reasons. While the president had a few die-hard defenders, between July 28 and 30 the Judiciary Committee voted 27–11 to begin impeachment proceedings in the full House on August 19. The committee had voted on three of five counts: (1) obstruction of justice through the payment of hush money to witnesses, lying, and withholding of evidence; (2) defiance of a congressional subpoena for the remaining tapes; and (3) the use of the CIA, the FBl, and the IRS (Nixon had pushed the Internal Revenue Service to examine the tax returns of his "enemies") to undermine the Constitution and deprive Americans of their rights.

With the latest Gallup poll revealing an all-time low for the president (his approval rating had dwindled to 24 percent, while his disapproval rating had skyrocketed to 63 percent), Nixon had little room to maneuver. The results of a Harris poll were even worse: 66–27 percent in favor of impeachment. Still, Nixon's natural instinct was to fight on. He had weathered other crises in his political past. In the early morning of July 31, a restless president sat down at 3:50 A.M. and for almost three hours listed the pros and cons of what would be best for him, his family, and the country. By morning, when he had finished making his notes, he wrote, "End career as a fighter." He would take his case to the Senate, where the Constitution gave him the right to a trial following a bill of impeachment delivered by the House. However, the prospects for victory were bleak—Senate Republican leader Hugh Scott of Pennsylvania had already informed Vice President Ford that conviction in the Senate was a virtual certainty.

There was still one more shocker before this drama of Shakespearean proportions was to play itself out: the "smoking gun." When Alexander Haig read the transcript of Nixon's conversation with H. R. Haldeman of June 23, 1972, Haig knew the ballgame was over. That tape answered Tennessee senator Howard Baker's key question: "What did you know and when did you know it?" It showed that, in this very early discussion with his closest aide, President Nixon knew a lot more than he ever let on.

On the tape Nixon asked Haldeman if John Mitchell knew about the Watergate break-in. "I think so," Haldeman answered. Nixon then asked if Mitchell had persuaded G. Gordon Liddy ("who must be a little nuts!" he said) to take part. Responding to the possibility that the FBI would question people in the White House, Nixon ordered, "Play it tough. That's the way they play it and that's the way we are going to play it." Nixon then instructed Haldeman to cover up the Watergate problem by calling the CIA and telling them that further inquiry might lead to "the whole Bay of Pigs thing." He also told Haldeman to tell the CIA that Watergate "is a comedy of errors" and that the CIA should call the FBI and say, "Don't go further into this case (,) period!" Assessing this evidence, Stanley I. Kutler wrote in *The Wars of Watergate,* "the President knew. He knew that he had instigated a cover-up and thus had participated in an obstruction of justice almost from the outset of events."

Following the release of the June 23 transcript, Haig told the president, "I just don't see how we can survive this one." The next day, August 1, Nixon told his chief of staff that he intended to resign. As Nixon later said obliquely, "If the June 23 tape was not explainable, I could not very well expect the staff to try to explain and defend it."

The Nixon family: standing, left to right, Mr. and Mrs. David (Julie Nixon) Eisenhower and Mr. and Mrs. Edward (Tricia Nixon) Cox; seated, President Nixon and First Lady Pat Nixon   (Richard Nixon Library)

Rejecting a last-minute appeal for a pardon by his ex-aide H. R. Haldeman, Nixon prepared himself to resign the presidency. On the night of August 7 Rose Mary Woods informed the Nixon family, who had gathered in the White House solarium, "Your father has decided to resign." Nixon arrived shortly afterward and tried to comfort his sobbing daughters. Stoic to the end, Pat Nixon held back any emotions she might have been feeling. Next to arrive was White House photographer Ollie Atkins, who had been summoned by the president to take some last-minute pictures of the family together in the White House. Mrs. Nixon politely tried to send Atkins away but the president insisted that he "take a few shots." At about eight o'clock Nixon summoned Henry Kissinger. Together they had made more history than any team in the long foreign policy history of the nation. In recent weeks Kissinger had been very unhappy, even though Nixon had nominated him to be secretary of state and his appointment had been confirmed the previous September. Watergate had turned his foreign policy strategy into a shambles. Like the rest of the people close to Nixon in the last year, Kissinger realized that the government had been operating in a virtual state of paralysis.

With Kissinger, Nixon could no longer hold back his pent-up emotions. The president broke down sobbing. He asked Kissinger, a nonobservant Jew, to get down on his knees with him and pray. Kissinger knelt. Nixon pounded his fist on the carpet and, still sobbing, said, "What have I done? What has happened?"

On Thursday, August 8, Nixon informed the country in a televised address that he was resigning the presidency. After the speech, Kissinger waited for Nixon in the corridor and said, "Mr. President, after most of your major speeches in this office we have walked together back to your house. I would be honored to walk with you again tonight."

Kissinger spoke sadly and softly as he and Nixon walked together past the darkened Rose Garden. He told Nixon that he thought that he had given a great speech and that history would judge him as one of the great presidents. Nixon turned to Kissinger and said, "That depends, Henry, on who writes the history."

10

FACING HISTORY
Richard Nixon's Last Crisis

> "History will treat me fairly. Historians probably won't, because most historians are on the left."
>
> —Richard Nixon, *Time*, April 2, 1990

> "'But he has nothing on!' at last cried all the people. The Emperor writhed, for he knew it was true."
>
> —Hans Christian Andersen, *The Emperor's New Clothes*

In his 1973 comedy *Sleeper,* Woody Allen plays Miles Monroe, a man who is frozen in 1973 and wakes up again in the 21st century. While watching videotapes with bewildered futuristic social scientists, the Woody Allen character points out that they are seeing Richard Nixon. The scientists apparently have never heard of Nixon and only seem to know that he did something very terrible since all historical traces of him have been erased. The bemused Monroe says, "Yes, he was actually President of the United States but when he left the White House the Secret Service used to count the silverware."

When President Ronald Reagan sent all of the living ex-presidents (Gerald Ford, Jimmy Carter, and Richard Nixon) to represent the United States at Egyptian president Anwar Sadat's funeral in 1981, Republican senator Bob Dole took the opportunity to make a wisecrack at Nixon's expense. "There they go," Dole said—"See-No-Evil, Speak-No-Evil, and Evil."

In the 1984 Robert Altman film *Secret Honor,* actor Philip Baker Hall, who bears an uncanny resemblance to Nixon, portrayed a suicidal ex-president stumbling around his study in a drunken stupor as he raves and shouts vile obscenities beneath the portraits of Woodrow Wilson, George Washington, Dwight Eisenhower, Abraham Lincoln, and Henry Kissinger. In Altman's film, Nixon exists in a paranoid world, surrounded by racks of endlessly flickering TV screens and surveillance cameras. As he gets drunker and drunker Nixon attempts to explain Watergate by some fanciful linkage to the Kennedy assassination and the Bay of Pigs fiasco.

With few exceptions, the historical image of Richard Nixon in American popular culture is far from what Nixon could have imagined or desired. As he observed with some pain in 1990, looking back on the aftermath of his resignation:

> The pounding continued unrelentingly. I was the favorite butt of jokes on the talk shows. Hundreds of columns attacked me. A number of anti-Nixon books were published. Those by critics I understood. Those by friends I found hard to take.
>
> The Rose Bowl game in 1975 was interrupted on television by an announcement of the conviction of John Mitchell and my other top aides. I could no longer even take refuge in my favorite avocation, watching sports on television.
>
> It was not enough for my critics to say that I had made terrible mistakes. They seemed driven to prove that I represented the epitome of evil itself.

When Gerald Ford took the oath of office three minutes after Richard Nixon's resignation went into effect, he told the nation, "Our long national nightmare is over." On September 8, 1974, against the counsel of many advisers and political observers, Ford issued a pardon to Nixon, removing any possibility that he could be prosecuted for crimes relating to the Watergate cover-up. Although he was unfairly accused of making a "deal" with Nixon before taking office, Ford probably acted out of a sense of decency and humanity. Alexander Haig had reportedly suggested that unless Ford issued a full pardon, Nixon might suffer "a personal and national tragedy." Haig later denied this, but there were other reports filtering back to the Ford White House that Nixon looked terrible and was deeply depressed. Clearly, some people close to Nixon worried that he was suicidal. After the pardon Nixon released a statement saying in part,

> I was wrong in not acting more decisively and more forthrightly in dealing with Watergate, particularly when it reached the stage of judicial proceedings and grew from a political scandal into a national tragedy.

That was all he would ever say about his complicity in the affair. As a result, the image of Richard Nixon took an endless public savaging. Nixon lived for 20 years after he left the White House. He would spend most of that time, after an initial bout with illness, gloom, and depression, engaged in what might accurately be described as his "seventh crisis"—a calculated campaign for resurrection.

In 1978 Nixon published his memoirs, *RN: The Memoirs of Richard Nixon*. After the book received relatively positive reviews, Nixon went from his reclusive exile to the campaign trail once again—only this time he was campaigning for American public opinion and acceptance as America's elder statesman.

In the ensuing years Nixon was to once again accept speaking engagements from around the country, informal invitations to the White House for chats with his successors, and widely publicized overseas trips to France, England, Russia, and China. Over the years Nixon received warm receptions in these and other foreign capitals. In 1979, amidst many complaints, President Carter invited Nixon to a state dinner for Chinese deputy prime minister Deng Xiaoping. The Chinese, who held Nixon in high regard, had insisted that the former president be present and even threatened to have Deng visit Nixon in San Clemente if Carter refused their request.

In 1981, after attending President Anwar Sadat's funeral, Nixon was flown to Jidda, where he was hosted for dinner by the Saudi royal family, including King Khalid and Crown Prince Fahd. He then went on to Amman, Jordan, for a banquet with King Hussein. Wherever he traveled, the former president was treated with all the dignity and respect that befitted an important former world leader.

His ultimate success in this quest is testimony to his resilience, toughness, and instinct for survival. Lesser men might have gone into seclusion, never to be heard from again, or actually gone mad, as does the Nixon character in *Secret Honor*. But as Stephen E. Ambrose writes in *Nixon: Ruin and Recovery*, "What had seemed impossible in the summer of 1974 had happened by the summer of 1990. Nixon was respectable, even honored, certainly admired. As with his earlier comebacks and successes, there was no mystery or miracle involved. He had planned the campaign, and executed it, carefully and wisely."

Nixon did his best to secure an image as America's elder statesman and a valued adviser to those presidents who followed him. In a way, Nixon was more successful than even he could have initially dreamed. Only six years after resigning in disgrace and accepting the embarrassing pardon, Nixon was back as an influential force in the new administration of Ronald Reagan. Reagan's biographer Lou Cannon writes,

> Nixon's influence on key appointments and even some of Reagan's strategic decisions is one of the untold stories. . . . Reagan told Nixon in a post-election telephone conversation that he would welcome any advice he had to give. Nixon, never lacking for an agenda, responded with alacrity. He composed an eleven-page memo that was hand-delivered to Reagan in Washington. . . . The memo made an effective case for the political strategy Reagan would follow in his first months in office. It made an even more effective case for the men that Reagan would name as secretary of state, director of central intelligence, attorney general and other positions.

Since his resignation, many full-scale biographies have been written about the life and presidency of Nixon. Most have been highly critical and very negative. Presidential scholar Stephen E. Ambrose is fairly representative of this anti-Nixon school of historiography. His comprehensive three-volume biography, which ends with Nixon's triumphant appearance at the dedication of the Nixon library and birthplace in Yorba Linda,

California, on July 19, 1990, is a tough but fair and comprehensive analysis of Nixon and his longevity in American public life. To Ambrose, Nixon was "not a great leader." Instead, he sees Nixon as a man "infected by self-pity" because of his childhood poverty and because, unlike his archrivals Kennedy and Rockefeller, he had to continually struggle for respect and success in the political world. In Ambrose's judgment, "Nixon overdid his boyhood experiences to elicit sympathy." Ambrose views Nixon as "the angriest American President" in history—an anger that, when uncurbed, led to Watergate and the politics of disaster.

However, Ambrose does not limit himself to generalizations about Nixon. He examines the Nixon domestic record and again concludes that "Nixon has no claim to greatness." In Ambrose's estimation Nixon might have achieved substantial reform in crucial areas like welfare, national health insurance, government reorganization, and revenue sharing with the states had he remained in office and given undivided presidential attention to these matters. But because of the intrusion of Watergate, Ambrose believes, "in each case he failed."

In foreign policy Ambrose also gives Nixon a failing grade. He charges Nixon with concentrating too much of his attention on Watergate while allowing North Vietnam to grow so bold that by 1975, after Nixon had resigned, a spring military offensive led to the fall of Saigon. Writing 10 years after the fact, Nixon blamed Congress for this, saying, "We won the war in Vietnam, but lost the peace." But Ambrose points out that Nixon, had he remained in office, could have obtained funds from Congress to prop up a faltering South Vietnam in 1975. Ambrose even diminishes the important opening to China that many Richard Nixon loyalists point to as his major achievement, writing, "Because Nixon resigned, the full promise of his opening to China has not been realized."

An opposing point of view is advanced by Joan Hoff in her 1994 study *Nixon Reconsidered*. This revisionist approach tries to balance the books in assessing the Nixon presidency. Hoff builds her case by arguing that Nixon's 2,027 days in the White House "must be viewed other than through the scrim of Watergate." Citing important and creative approaches to complex domestic problems, Hoff views the Nixon years in a much more positive light.

Hoff contends that Nixon's "New Federalism," designed to take traditional politics out of domestic legislation, never received the attention it deserved from a hostile press. She cites the Nixon administration's many domestic achievements: the continuing desegregation of southern schools; support for affirmative action as evidenced by "the Philadelphia Plan" (with "set-asides" for minority construction workers); strong environmental policies; continued support for the Small Business Administration through the creation in 1969 of the Office of Minority Business Enterprise (OMBE); sensitivity in dealing with Native American land claims in Alaska and with the dangerously explosive violence that cropped up in 1973 at Wounded Knee, on the Pine Ridge Sioux Reservation in South Dakota. Nixon actually increased the budget of the Bureau of Indian Affairs (BIA) by 214 percent—an increase of $300 million in two years. And funds spent to improve the health of American Indians doubled in Nixon's first term.

In Hoff's view Nixon was an activist leader in civil rights as well, and she calls him "a stronger supporter of civil rights than Eisenhower, Kennedy, or Johnson." As Hoff notes,

> The Nixon administration desegregated southern schools; significantly increased funding for the enforcement of both group and individual civil rights; achieved court approval of goals in hiring practices rather than quotas; and clearly transformed the power and responsibility for civil rights to a court-enforced approach based on recommendations of permanent government affirmative agencies within the executive branch. . . . Nixon's advances in civil and political rights for women and minorities far outweighed those of his predecessors.

In foreign policy, however, which Hoff calls "Nixinger Diplomacy," Nixon gets less-than-glowing reviews. Hoff concludes that "Nixon's diplomatic legacy is weaker than he and many others have maintained." Like other critics, Hoff cites the failed peace in Vietnam and points out that the shuttle diplomacy of Henry Kissinger "ended up more show than substance" in the Middle East. In addition, she says that Nixon had no substantive Third World policy and that the delicate detente with the Soviet Union achieved by Nixon soon floundered under successors such as Jimmy Carter and Ronald Reagan. And while

Nixon's opening to China has lasted, China remains a major problem area for U.S. foreign policy.

The battle between the Nixon detractors and the Nixon supporters will continue for many years to come. No president in American history left behind such an available public record, and future generations will have ample opportunity to form their own judgments.

Nixon's most immediate legacy is the fact that he brought the institution of the American presidency to an all-time low—a low from which the nation and the presidency have not yet recovered. As George Reedy noted in his book *The Twilight of the Presidency,* Nixon "left the nation with a sense of distrust for the office itself rather than just for the men who occupied it."

When Richard Nixon died on April 22, 1994, four days after suffering a massive stroke, there was an appropriate urge throughout the country to recall the best about him. The Reverend Billy Graham, who officiated at the funeral service at the Nixon Library, said, "I think he was one of the most misunderstood men, and I think he was one of the greatest men of the century."

Taking a more objective view the day after Nixon's death, the *Washington Post* offered this assessment:

> He was to politics what Sinatra has been to music: Permanent, easy to parody, a mixed bag of genius and ugliness and incomparable endurance. And to paraphrase Sinatra, America got Nixon under its skin, and once he got there, he polarized and galvanized, frightened and thrilled. He got into peoples' hearts and spleens; snippets of his language lodged in your head like a popular tune.

Former White House speechwriter William Safire tried to explain the Nixon enigma by saying that nobody ever saw the real Nixon—not even his own beloved family. Safire compared Nixon to a seven-layer cake, noting that everyone with whom Nixon dealt saw a different layer, which convinced them that they had seen the real Nixon. Thus, in Safire's view, there were many Richard Nixons.

The media loved to play on this theme as they endlessly created "Old Nixons" and "New Nixons." In the final analysis, however, there was only one Nixon—a man strangely unsuited to the profession he chose for his life's work: politics. Politics is about people, and Richard M. Nixon was, for the most part, uncomfortable with most people. Historically, such men have usually been rejected by the voters when they have sought high public office. But this was not to be Richard Nixon's political fate. In the end, after gaining the acceptance he had sought for so long, it was Nixon who rejected the American people by betraying their sacred trust.

Henry Kissinger may have come closest to capturing the tragic puzzle of the real Richard Nixon when he asked journalist Hugh Sidey, "Can you imagine what this man would have been had somebody loved him?" "What do you mean?" Sidey asked. "Had somebody in his life cared for him. I don't think anybody ever did, not his parents, not his peers," Kissinger said. Then he added, "He would have been a great, great man had somebody loved him."

FURTHER READING

Students who visit Southern California should put the Richard Nixon Library and Birthplace on their itinerary. While all presidential libraries are built with private funds, the Nixon Library was built and is operated without any taxpayer support. This private museum and research facility houses the important prepresidential papers of Richard Nixon. The museum is open daily and on Sundays. Interested scholars and researchers should write in advance to the Richard Nixon Library, 18001 Yorba Linda Boulevard, Yorba Linda, California, 92886; or call 714-993-3393. Also see Susan Naulty, "Creating an Archives at the Richard Nixon Library and Birthplace," *Government Information Quarterly,* Vol. 11, No. 1, 1993.

Richard Nixon: The Early Years

There has not yet been a first-rate study dealing with Richard Nixon's childhood and his relationship with his parents and brothers. Some of the earliest works, written before his first campaign for the presidency, still stand up to historical scrutiny. They include William Costello, *The Facts About Nixon: An Unauthorized Biography* (New York: Viking Press, 1960); Earl Mazo, *Richard Nixon: A Political and Personal Portrait* (New York: Harper & Row, 1959); and Earl Mazo and Stephen Hess, *Richard Nixon: A Political Portrait* (New York: Harper & Row, 1968).

The Hiss Case

Alger Hiss died in 1996 still protesting his innocence. Because of the steady flow of information from the Soviet archives and from declassified U.S. intelligence documents, most scholars now conclude otherwise. It is a controversy that will undoubtedly go on.

The best analysis of the Hiss case to date is Allen Weinstein, *Perjury: The Hiss-Chambers Case* (New York: Knopf, 1978, revised 1997). For views from both sides, students should also see Whittaker Chambers, *Witness* (New York: Random House, 1952), and Alger Hiss, *In the Court of Public Opinion* (New York: Knopf, 1957). For Richard Nixon's view, see *Six Crises* (New York: Simon & Schuster, 1990). Also see Meyer A. Zeligs, M.D., *Friendship and Fratricide: An Analysis of Whittaker Chambers and Alger Hiss* (New York: Viking Press, 1967).

Nixon the Candidate: The Campaigns for the Presidency

The election of 1960, considered by many to be the last exciting presidential race in this century, is best told by Theodore H. White in his classic *The Making of the President 1960* (New York: Atheneum, 1961). This is still the best of what became a quadrennial publishing event until 1972. Students should also see Theodore H. White, *The Making of the President 1968* (New York: Atheneum, 1969), and *The Making of the President 1972* (New York: Atheneum, 1973). For what *Newsweek* called "the political Bible of the Nixon era," see Kevin P. Phillips, *The Emerging Republican Majority* (Garden City, N.Y.: Doubleday, 1970). For a fascinating look inside the Nixon campaign of 1968, see Joe McGinnis, *The Selling of the President 1968* (New York: Trident Press, 1969).

On the Couch: Nixon versus the Psychohistorians

Richard Nixon despised being analyzed by psychologists, psychiatrists, and psychohistorians. To the end of his life, Nixon railed against the fact that people who had never met him or even spoken to him could have the audacity to write about what made him tick. Nevertheless, there are a number of first-rate studies on Nixon that employ a psychohistorical approach. Among these are David Abrahamsen, *Nixon vs. Nixon: An Emotional Tragedy* (New York: Farrar, Straus and Giroux, 1977); Fawn M. Brodie, *Richard Nixon: The Shaping of His Character* (Cambridge, Mass.: Harvard University Press, 1983); Eli S. Chesen, M.D., *President Nixon's Psychiatric Profile* (New York: Peter H. Wyden, 1973); and an interesting study that predicted Nixon's destructive behavior before Watergate, Bruce Mazlish, *In Search of Nixon: A Psychohistorical Inquiry* (Baltimore: Penguin Books, 1973).

Richard Nixon, Vietnam, and Cambodia

The complex nature of America's long "adventure" in Southeast Asia can best be explored through the early work of Bernard B. Fall, *The Two Viet-Nams: A Political and Military Analysis* (New York: Praeger, 1966). Fall, a journalist on the scene, was killed in Vietnam in 1967. The best overall scholarly treatments are Stanley Karnow, *Vietnam: A History* (New York: Viking, 1983); and Frances Fitzgerald, *Fire in the Lake: The Vietnamese and the Americans in Vietnam* (Boston: Atlantic-Little, Brown, 1972). Also see Nyguyen Tien Hung and Jerrold L. Schecter, *The Palace File: Vietnam Secret Documents* (New York: Harper & Row, 1986) for new data on the secret correspondence between Presidents Nixon and Ford and the president of South Vietnam. For an excellent overview of the American cold war foreign policy that led to Vietnam, see Walter LaFeber, *America, Russia, and the Cold War 1945–1984* (New York: Knopf, 1985). Also see William Shawcross, *Sideshow: Kissinger, Nixon and the Destruction of Cambodia* (New York: Simon & Schuster, 1979).

The President's Men: On Nixon, the Presidency, and Watergate

Valuable insights into Nixon the man and the president are offered by many people who were closest to him in the White House. Students should see H. R. Haldeman, *The Ends of Power* (New York: Times Books, 1978) and *The Haldeman Diaries: Inside the Nixon White House* (New York: Putnam, 1994); John Dean, *Blind Ambition: The White House Years* (New York: Simon & Schuster, 1976); John Ehrlichman, *Witness to Power: The Nixon Years* (New York: Simon & Schuster, 1982); Herbert G. Klein, *Making It Perfectly Clear* (Garden City, N.Y.: Doubleday, 1980); Jeb Stuart Magruder, *An American Life: One Man's Road to Watergate* (New York: Atheneum, 1974); Raymond Price, *With Nixon* (New York: Viking, 1977); William Safire, *Before the Fall* (Garden City, N.Y.: Doubleday, 1975); and Henry Kissinger, *White House Years* (Boston: Little,

Brown, 1979) and *Years of Upheaval* (Boston: Little, Brown, 1982).

Biographies and History

The excellent three-volume work by Stephen E. Ambrose, *Nixon: The Education of a Politician, 1913–1962* (New York: Simon & Schuster, 1987), *Nixon: The Triumph of a Politician, 1962–1972* (New York: Simon & Schuster, 1989), and *Nixon: Ruin and Recovery, 1973–1990* (New York: Simon & Schuster, 1991) forms the most comprehensive study of Nixon to date. Students should also see Joan Hoff, *Nixon Reconsidered* (New York: Basic Books, 1994) for an opposing point of view. Also see Roger Morris, *Richard Milhous Nixon: The Rise of an American Politician* (New York: Holt, 1990); Garry Wills, *Nixon Agonistes: The Crisis of the Self-Made Man* (Boston: Houghton Mifflin, 1970); Herbert S. Parmet, *Richard Nixon and His America* (Boston: Little, Brown, 1990); and a recent biography by a member of the British parliament who is a Nixon admirer, Jonathan Aitken, *Nixon: A Life* (Washington, D.C.: Regnery, 1993).

For students and young readers looking for biographies of Nixon written specifically for young adults, there are Rebecca Larsen, *Richard Nixon: Rise and Fall of a President* (New York: Franklin Watts, 1991); C. Peter Ripley, *Richard Nixon* (New York: Chelsea House, 1988); Roger Barr, *Richard Nixon* (San Diego: Lucent Books, 1992); and Rebecca Stefoff, *Richard M. Nixon: Thirty-seventh President of the United States* (Ada, Okla.: Garrett Educational Corp., 1990).

Richard Nixon: Reflections and Foreign Policy

Richard Nixon had an excellent mind and was a good writer. He published ten books after leaving the presidency. His writings offer much insight into his life and public service, though Nixon was often self-serving in dealing with his own shortcomings and his complicity in Watergate. Nixon's best books include Richard Nixon, *Six Crises* (New York: Simon & Schuster, 1990); *RN: The Memoirs of Richard Nixon* (New York: Grosset and Dunlap, 1978); and *In the Arena: A Memoir of Victory, Defeat and Renewal* (New York: Simon & Schuster, 1990). Interested readers should also see other books by Richard

Nixon: *The Real War* (New York: Warner Books, 1980); *Leaders* (New York: Simon & Schuster, 1990); *No More Vietnams* (New York: Avon Books, 1985); *Real Peace* (New York: Simon & Schuster, 1990); *1999: Victory Without War* (New York: Simon & Schuster, 1988); *Seize the Moment: America's Challenge in a One-Superpower World* (New York: Simon & Schuster, 1992); and *Beyond Peace* (New York: Random House, 1994).

Watergate

Watergate will continue to define Nixon's presidency for the foreseeable future. Two good general studies are Theodore H. White, *Breach of Faith: The Fall of Richard Nixon* (New York: Atheneum, 1975); and Fred Emery, *Watergate: The Corruption of American Politics and the Fall of Richard Nixon* (New York: Simon & Schuster, 1994). Students should also see the two books by the pair of reporters who caused the Nixon White House so much consternation in 1973: Carl Bernstein and Bob Woodward, *All the President's Men* (New York: Warner, 1975); and Bob Woodward and Carl Bernstein, *The Final Days* (New York: Simon & Schuster, 1976). The best and toughest historical analysis of Watergate to date is Stanley I. Kutler, *The Wars of Watergate: The Last Crisis of Richard Nixon* (New York: Knopf, 1990). Students should not overlook the readily available printed transcripts of Nixon's taped presidential conversations. They can be found in *The White House Transcripts* (New York: Bantam Books, 1974); in *The Fall of a President,* by the staff of the *Washington Post* (New York: Dell, 1974); and in *Hearings Before the Committee on the Judiciary, House of Representatives . . . to Impeach Richard M. Nixon, President of the United States of America* (Washington, D.C.: Government Printing Office, 1974). This document contains eight recorded presidential conversations. Also valuable and of interest: J. Anthony Lukas, *Nightmare: The Underside of the Nixon Years* (New York: Bantam Books, 1977); and Len Colodny and Robert Gettlin, *Silent Coup: The Removal of a President* (New York: St. Martin's, 1991).

Documents, Oral Histories, and Collected Essays

An excellent and useful collection of materials that includes Nixon's personal and private memorandums to many of his key staffers can be found in Bruce Oudes, editor, *From the President: Richard Nixon's Secret Files* (New York: Harper & Row, 1989). For an insightful volume of oral history interviews dealing with the Nixon years, see Gerald S. Strober and Deborah Hart Strober, *Nixon: An Oral History of His Presidency* (New York: HarperCollins, 1994). Also see Lloyd C. Gardner, editor, *The Great Nixon Turnaround: America's New Foreign Policy in the Post-Liberal Era* (New York: Franklin Watts, 1973) for a focus on foreign policy.

The Modern Presidency

While many studies of the presidency have been written, there are three excellent books that analyze the influence of Nixon on the modern presidency. They are James David Barber, *The Presidential Character: Predicting Performance in the White House* (Englewood Cliffs, N.J.: Prentice Hall, 1977); Richard E. Neustadt, *Presidential Power: The Politics of Leadership with Reflections on Johnson and Nixon* (New York: Wiley, 1976); and George E. Reedy, *The Twilight of the Presidency: From Johnson to Reagan* (New York: Meridian, 1988).

Postwar America in the Age of Richard Nixon

For an excellent overview of the postwar America in which Nixon cut his political teeth, see Eric F. Goldman, *The Crucial Decade—and After: America, 1945–1960* (New York: Vintage Books, 1960). There are a number of first-rate studies dealing with the 1960s up to and through Nixon's 1968 triumph. They include Todd Gitlin, *The Sixties: Years of Hope, Days of Rage* (New York: Bantam, 1987); Allen J. Matusow, *The Unraveling of America: A History of Liberalism in the 1960s* (New York: Harper & Row, 1984); William L. O'Neill, *Coming Apart: An Informal History of America in the 1960s* (Chicago: Quadrangle, 1971); and Jonathan Schell, *The Time of Illusion* (New York: Vintage, 1975).

Index

Italic page numbers indicate illustrations.
Boldface page numbers indicate major treatments.

A

Acheson, Dean 26, 28
Agnew, Spiro T. 79, 87, 119–20
anticommunism 16, 17–18, **21–30**, 33, **44–46,** 85, 89 *See also* House Committee on Un-American Activities
antiwar movement 74, 76, 77, 78, 79–80, 83–84, 85, 90–96, 98, 99, 105

B

Barker, Bernard L. 103
Bay of Pigs crisis 68, 125
Bernstein, Carl 104, 108
Black Panthers 92
Bork, Robert 118, 120
Brown, Pat 69, 70, 71
Brownell, Herbert, Jr. 33, 34, 35, 37
Butterfield, Alexander 117

C

Cambodia 85, 86, 90, 91, 93
Camp David 115, 121
Camp David Accords 119
Carter, Jimmy 128, 130, 133
Castro, Fidel 55, 68
Central Intelligence Agency (CIA) xiii, 55, 68, 90, 99, 103, 105, 110, 112, 125–26
Chambers, Whittaker 22, **23–26**
"Checkers" speech **39–41,** 43–44
Chile 100
China, People's Republic of xi, 27, 29, 85, 100, 130, 132, 134

Chotiner, Murray 17, 27, 28, 35, 37, 38, 41, 42, 70, 80
Churchill, Winston 21, 73–74
civil rights movement 62, 64, 75–76
cold war 21–22, 26, 85, 89, 100
Colson, Charles 104, 105, 106, 107, 115, 116
Committee to Re-elect the President (CREEP) 103, 105–7
Congress of Industrial Organizations (CIO) 17–18
"containment" policy 23
Cox, Archibald 118
Cox, Tricia Nixon 38, 39, 67, 68, 69, 70, *126,* 127
Cronin, John F., Father 22–23, 26
Cuban Missile Crisis 71

D

Daley, Richard 54, 66
Dean, John 106, 108, 113–15, 116, 117, 121
Democratic National Convention (1960) 54
Democratic National Convention (1968) 79–80
Democratic Republic of Vietnam 85 *See also* North Vietnam
Deng Xiaoping 130
Dewey, Thomas E. 33, 34, 37, 38
domino theory 90
Douglas, Helen Gahagan 27–30
Downey, Sheridan 27
Duke University 8
Dulles, Allen 68
Dulles, John Foster 47, 48

INDEX

E

Education and Labor Committee (U.S. House of Representatives) 21, 22
Ehrlichman, John 94, 105, 114, 115–16, 124
Eisenhower, Dwight David (U.S. president)
  1952 presidential campaign 30, 33–35, 37–44
  and Nixon's 1960 presidential campaign 51
  and Nixon's 1962 gubernatorial campaign 68, 71
  illnesses 46–47
Eisenhower, Julie Nixon 38, 67, 68, 69, 70, 91, *126*, 127
election years
  1946 18
  1948 27, 30
  1950 **27–30**, 32
  1952 30, **32–44**
  1956 47
  1960 48, **49–65**, 66–67
  1962 68–72
  1964 73
  1966 73
  1968 74–81
  1972 100, 101–9
Ellsberg, Daniel 99–100, 105, 123, 124
Ervin, Sam 114, 118

F

Federal Bureau of Investigation (FBI) xiii, 8, 22, 99, 105, 107, 110, 117, 125–26
Fielding, Lewis 105, 123, 124
"fifth column" 33 *See also* anticommunism
Ford, Gerald R. 120, 125, 128, 129, 130

G

Goldwater, Barry ix, 73, 81
Gonzalez, Virgilio R. 103
Gray, L. Patrick 108, 114–15
Great Depression 8

H

Hagerty, James 37, 40, 46
Haig, Alexander x, 118, 121, 125, 126, 129–30
Haldeman, H. R. (Bob) 56, 95, 96, 98–99, 107, 113, 114, 115–16, 117, 121, 125, 127
Herblock (cartoonist) 121
Hiss, Alger **24–26,** 27, 31
Ho Chi Minh 85, 86, 90
Ho Chi Minh Trail 90
Hoover, J. Edgar 8, 99
House Committee on Un-American Activities (HUAC) 21–22, **23–26**
House Judiciary Committee 121, 123, 124–25
Humphrey, Hubert H. xi, 53, 78, 79–80, 81, 102
Hunt, E. Howard 103–4, 105–6, 107, 113–14, 114–15
Huston, Tom Charles 105

I

Internal Revenue Service (IRS) xiii, 125

J

Jaworski, Leon 120, 121, 123
Jobe, Ola Welch 7
Johnson, Lyndon Baines 51, 54, 71, 73, 74, 75, 76, 77, 78, 81, 87, 89, 90, 95, 102, 120
Justice Department (U.S.) 16

K

Kennedy, Edward M. 101–2, *101*
Kennedy, Jacqueline *64*, 67, 73
Kennedy, John F. *52, 61, 64, 69*
  assassination 73, 97
  debates with Nixon 57–61
  elected to Congress 19
  1960 presidential campaign 51, 53–54, 57–62
  and Vietnam War 86–87
  view of Nixon's personality 55
  war record 13
Kennedy, Joseph P. 7, 51, 63
Kennedy, Robert 54, 62, 77–78
Kennedy, Rose 7

Kent State killings 91–92, 93
Kersten, Charles 22
Khrushchev, Nikita 48, 51, 55
King, Coretta 62
King, Martin Luther, Jr. 62, 63, 75–76, *75*
Kinoy, Arthur 122–23
Kissinger, Henry x, 83, 88–89, 90, 94, 99, 100–1, 111–12, *111,* 127, 133
Kopechne, Mary Jo 101–2
Korean War 27, 29
Krause, Allison 92
Krogh, Egil ("Bud") 94

L

Laos 85, 86
Liddy, G. Gordon 103, 105–6, 107, 125
Lindsay, John 79, 93
Lodge, Henry Cabot 96
Los Angeles Times 30, 43, 114

M

Magruder, Jeb Stuart 99, 114, 115
Marcantonio, Vito 28–29
Martin, Joe 21
Martinez, Eugenio R. 103, 112
McCaffrey, Edward J. 13
McCarthy, Eugene 75, 77, 78
McCarthy, Joseph 28, 44–46, 48
McCord, James A. 103, 112–13
McGovern, George 102–3, 107, 108
McNamara, Robert 86, 99
Meir, Golda 119
Miami Herald 104, 112
Mitchell, John 82–83, 106, 114, 115, 116, 125, 129
Muskie, Edmund 80, 102

N

National Security Agency (NSA) 99
Native Americans 133
New Deal 8, 17, 20, 51
Ngo Dinh Diem 86
Nixon, Arthur (brother of President Nixon) 1, 5
Nixon, Donald (brother of President Nixon) 1, *2*

Nixon, Edward (brother of President Nixon) 1
Nixon, Frank (father of President Nixon) 1, *2,* **3,** 9
Nixon, Hannah Milhous (mother of President Nixon) 1, *2,* **3–4,** 5–7, 9, 10, 37
Nixon, Harold (brother of President Nixon) 1, **2,** 5, 7
Nixon, Julie (daughter of President Nixon) *See* Eisenhower, Julie Nixon
Nixon, Mudge, Rose, Guthrie, and Alexander (law firm) 72
Nixon, Pat (U.S. first lady) 9, 12, 15, 21, 28, 39, *41,* 43, 44, 67, 68, 69, 70, 73, 79, *84, 126,* 127
Nixon, Richard M. 2, 6, *41, 45, 52, 61, 64, 69, 84, 88, 126*
  and antiwar movement 90–96
  and Army-McCarthy hearings 44–46
  attitudes on race 8
  attitudes toward women 28
  childhood 1–7
  as cold warrior 17–18, 22–23, 33, 44–46, 85, 88–89
  as congressman **20–27,** 29
  dark side of character 56–56, 62, 98–99, 109, 122, 132
  death 134
  in debates 7, 17–18, 48, 57–61
  education 7–8
  feelings toward Eisenhower 38, 42, 44, 55, 56, 57
  and Hiss-Chambers case **23–26,** 27, 28, 31, 44, 46
  marriage to Pat Ryan 9
  nicknames 14, 30
  1946 House campaign 115–19
  1950 Senate campaign 27–30
  1952 slush-fund scandal 35–44
    See also "Checkers" speech
  1960 presidential campaign 49–51, 54, 57–62
  1962 gubernatorial campaign 68–72
  1968 presidential campaign 74–81
  1972 presidential campaign 101, 103–8
  place in history 130–34
  poker-playing abilities 13, 52

and the press 29, 56, 62, 67, 70, 71, 98, 110, 118–19, 133
in private life 72–74, 129–30
public-speaking abilities 33
and Quakerism 3, 4, 7, 9, 10
relationship with John Kennedy 52–53
relationship with mother 4–7
resignation from presidency ix–x, 126–27
Six Crises 25, 46
as vice president x, 44–48, 50
and Vietnam War xi, 84–85, 87–96, 100, 110, 132, 133
visit to China 100–1
war record 10, 11
Nixon, Tricia (daughter of President Nixon) *See* Cox, Tricia Nixon
"Nixon doctrine" 88–89
Nixon Library 131
North Vietnam 86, 87, 91, 96, 103, 111, 132
Nuclear Weapons and Foreign Policy (Kissinger) 83

P

Parmet, Herbert S. 44, 49, 53
Peale, Norman Vincent 63
Pentagon Papers 99–100
Perry, Herman L. 11, 15, 20, 21
"pink sheet" 28–29
"plumbers" unit 104–106
political violence 79–80, 83, 91–93

R

racial unrest 74, 75–76, 83
Reagan, Ronald 70–71, 79, 128, 131, 133
Rebozo, Bebe 104, 116
"red scare" *See* anticommunism
Republican National Convention (1952) 35
Republican National Convention (1960) 55
Republican National Convention (1964) 73
Republican National Convention (1968) 79
Republic of Vietnam *See* South Vietnam
Ribicoff, Abraham 80

Richardson, Elliot 116, 118
RN: The Memoirs of Richard Nixon 116, 130
Rockefeller, Nelson A. 50, 54–55, 77, 78, 83
Rodino, Peter 123
Rogers, William 83
Romney, George 77
Roosevelt, Franklin D. 9, 17, 20, 51
Ruckelshaus, William 117, 118
Rusk, Dean 86
Ryan, Thelma Catherine ("Pat") *See* Nixon, Pat

S

St. Clair, James 123
Sanchez, Manuel (Manolo) 94, 95
Secret Honor (film) 129, 131
Senate Select Committee on Campaign Practices 114, 117, 121
Shriver, R. Sargent 102–3
Sirica, John 112, 121
Six Crises 25, 46
Sleeper (film) 128
South Vietnam 86, 90, 111
Soviet Union 21, 27, 55, 85, 100, 119, 133
Stalin, Joseph 21
Stassen, Harold 37
Stevenson, Adlai E. 36, 47, 48
Stripling, Robert 26
Students for a Democratic Society (SDS) 76, 92
Sturgis, Frank A. 103
Supreme Court (U.S.) 122–23, 124

T

Taft, Robert A. 33
Taft-Hartley Act 53
television
    "Checkers" speech 39–41
    and Nixon's 1968 presidential campaign 80–81
    and Watergate scandal 117, 118–19, 124
    Nixon-Kennedy debates 57–61
Tet offensive 74, 77
Thompson, Fred 117
Truman, Harry xiii, 20, 23, 25, 26, 27, 28, 29, 35, 49

U

U.S. v. U.S. District Court for the Eastern District of Michigan 122–23
urban violence 74, 75–76, 83, 92–93

V

Victory at Sea (film) 81
Viet Cong 86, 87
"Vietnamization" 89, 96
Vietnam War
  cost 84, 87–88
  early years 85
  Eisenhower administration policy toward 86
  Johnson administration policy toward 74, 76, 77, 87
  Kennedy administration policy toward 86–87
  Nixon administration policy toward 87–91, 93, 94, 95, 96, 100, 111, 132, 133
  Truman administration policy toward 85–86
Voorhis, Jerry 15–16, 17–18

W

Wallace, George C. 80, 81, 102
Washington Post ix, 104, 106, 112, 121
Watergate scandal
  and atmosphere of Nixon administration 96, 98–100
  burglary of Democratic National Committee headquarters at Watergate Hotel 103–4
  investigation into 110, 112, 114–15, 117, 118, 120–21, 123–26
  Nixon administration cover-up 107–8, 110, 112–15, 117–18
  Nixon tapes 117–18, 120–22, 123, 124–26
  and "plumbers" unit 104–6
  "Saturday night massacre" 118–19, 120
  "smoking gun" 125
Weathermen 92
White House Transcripts, The 121–23
Whittier, California 3, 8, 15, 35, 50
Whittier College 7–8, 9, 35
Woods, Rose Mary 42, 121, 127
Woodward, Bob 104, 108
World War II 9, 10, **11–15**, 16
Wounded Knee, South Dakota 133
Wright, Bewley, and Nixon 8–9

Y

Yippies (Youth International Party) 79
Yom Kippur War xi, 119
Yorba Linda, California xii, 1, 2, 131–32

Z

Ziegler, Ron 92, 94, 108, 121